DevOps Mindset in Software Development

DevOps Mindset in Software Development

From Apprentice to Journeyman

Dr. Bernhard Scheffold

THAUMAZO PUBLISHING

Imprint

DevOps Mindset in Software Development
From Apprentice to Journeyman
Original Edition 2025

Author:
Dr. Bernhard Scheffold

Publisher: thaumazo publishing
Caroline Helbing
Sondershauser Straße 103
12209 Berlin, Germany
www.thaumazo-publishing.com
(Production, Copy Editing, Graphic Design)

Cover Art: Adri Rossow

Typeset with: LaTeX, tex4ebook

Printed by:
Amazon Media EU S.à.r.l.
5 Rue Plaetis, L-2338 Luxembourg

Ingram Content Group UK Ltd,
Chapter House, Pitfield, Kiln Farm,
Milton Keynes MK11 3LW, UK

ISBNs:
Hardcover: 978-3-9827392-0-5
Paperback: 978-3-9827392-1-2
eBook: 978-3-9827392-2-9

Contents

Foreword v

Preface ix

How to Read this Book xiii

I Setting the Stage 1

1 Three Pillars of DevOps 3

1.1 Flow 4
1.2 Feedback 7
1.3 Continuous Improvement 8

2 Customer Orientation 11

2.1 Business Requirements 11
2.2 System Integration 12
2.3 Operations Issues 17

II The Road from Apprentice to Journeyman 21

3 Starting Point: Ignorance 23

4 First Level: Awareness 27

4.1 Wrong Assumptions 27
4.2 Becoming Aware 30
4.2.1 Unit Tests 30

4.2.2 Integration Tests 32
4.2.3 Acceptance Tests 35
4.2.4 Load Tests 35
4.2.5 PEN Tests 36
4.2.6 Monitoring 37
4.2.7 Logging 38
4.2.8 Reporting 39
4.2.9 Observability 40
4.2.10 Business Feedback 40

5 Second Level: Reactivity **45**
5.1 Mitigation 45
5.2 Analysis of Issues 48
5.2.1 Log File Analysis 51
5.2.2 Profiling 52
5.2.3 Query Plan Analysis 53
5.2.4 Memory Profiling 58
5.3 Blameless Postmortems 59
5.3.1 Sample Structure for Blameless Postmortem 61

6 Third Level: Preparedness **65**
6.1 Lean principles 65
6.1.1 Andon Cord 66
6.1.2 Kanban 67
6.1.3 Poka Yoke 68
6.1.4 Kaizen 69
6.1.5 Muda 69
6.2 Putting it to Work 71
6.2.1 Limit Work in Progress 72
6.2.2 Follow the Boy Scouts Rule 72
6.2.3 Avoid Coolness 73
6.2.4 Avoid Complexity 74
6.2.5 Avoid Flexibility 78

6.2.6 Make APIs Hard to Misuse 84
6.2.7 Don't Waste Resources 90
6.2.8 Limit Damage 93
6.2.9 Increase Analyzability 96
6.2.10 Increase Visibility 101
6.2.11 Increase Robustness 103
6.2.12 Respect your Legacy 107

III Evolution on the Organizational Level **111**

7 Overview **113**

8 High Performance Organizations **115**

9 Organizational Culture **119**

10 Values for Succeeding in Contract Projects **123**
10.1 Capability to Deliver 124
10.2 Quality 125
10.3 Focus on Value for the Customer 129
10.4 Vision 130
10.5 Transparency 131
10.6 Honesty 131
10.7 Modesty 132
10.8 Trust 133
10.9 Feedback 133
10.10 Ownership 134
10.11 Communication 136
10.12 Diligence 137
10.13 Clear responsibility 138

11 Evolution in Service Organizations by Example **139**
11.1 Web Shop for a Dealership 139
11.1.1 Project Setup 140

11.1.2 Project Evaluation 142
11.2 Web Shop for an Auction Platform 145
11.2.1 Project Setup 146
11.2.2 Project Evaluation 146
11.3 Web Shop for a Manufacturer 149
11.3.1 Project Setup 149
11.3.2 Project Evaluation 149

12 Closing Remarks **153**

List of Figures **157**

List of Tables **159**

Listings **161**

Bibliography **163**

Acknowledgments **165**

About the Author **167**

Foreword

Let's get right to the point: Why should you read this book? It does not even have 800 pages! Well, thankfully. It does not give you every detail about software development (it will point you to further sources) nor does it tell you which programming language you should use. And it is not an academic discussion of how to do software development. Instead, you need to read this book when you have to *deliver* real software solutions with real *value* for your customers. Delivering value through software should be a done deal today. But how many companies—creating or just using software—struggle greatly with exactly that?

If you work in the field of software production, you have probably realized that this is a very error-prone process. Looking back 30, 40 years—it would be easy to find examples where we seemingly did not improve at all today. Like the many times we have come up with another schema-less design just to go back to a schema later. Realizing, that without a schema definition, there is little to test for errors.

And the endless number of so-called "silver bullets" that have been touted over the years: new languages, new process models, none of them able to guarantee successful software solutions alone. Additionally, many misconceptions have accompanied software development over the years, like giving re-use absolute priority. Or forgetting time and budget in the quest for "flexibility".

This book discusses implementing and using DevOps which is just about the opposite of a "silver bullet". The DevOps mindset tears down organizational and mental silos to provide an end-to-end view of software delivery. The author shows that DevOps significantly improves software delivery, and he does this in a pragmatic way by giving many real-life examples from his 40-years of software development. These examples include not only technical and process know-how, but they let us understand the social and business context and the constraints we face when delivering software. And according to the author, we can do so even in complex multi-party and multi-contract situations, where the social components of DevOps really show their value.

So the book is not just a technical solution to the software delivery problem? Yes, it goes way beyond that.

Don't get me wrong: the book explains techniques to make components more reliable and robust. It explains integration problems and how they can be solved. It takes you through the process of setting up a pipeline for successful software delivery. But at the same time, it looks at the necessary interactions and communications between all involved parties, and it is futile to discuss what might be more important.

It includes clear examples, e.g., of bad user experience through bad API design. I've enjoyed using the example of the "confused indexer" in my 2nd grade lecture at the university. Typically, "user experience" problems are only discussed in the context of end-users. The confused indexer example shows that even professional software frequently suffers from badly designed internal APIs. Those APIs cause misunderstandings and are a frequent source for software defects. Personal responsibility in DevOps goes a long way beyond just finishing your part and throwing it over the fence to someone else.

The structure of the book is very simple and clear. The first part gives some technical background on DevOps (e.g., the important concept of establishing flow). The second part is about your journey through four different phases of DevOps implementation. And the last part is again a journey, but this time a journey through three types of organizations where you can learn to use the knowledge from the second part in difficult business settings.

This gets all accomplished in a concise, down-to-earth way. Stories from personal experience are used to let readers understand and remember the concepts. Many hints and links to more detailed information are given (you should really follow those links). But the book itself concentrates on what really counts, and that is a good thing!

I've mentioned misconceptions in the developer community, but management has its own. DevOps—if done right—has a profound effect on the whole company or organization. Breaking out of fixed organizational barriers by taking on a cross-sectional end-to-end view of software delivery is also a challenge for management. DevOps includes some very counter-intuitive wisdom about how to deal with a bad software delivery process.

The book avoids a nerdy or academic style and can be read by all people involved, not only by developers. In fact, it might be a good idea if you are eager to employ DevOps in your organization, that you give a copy of the book to your manager!

A few words about the author: You can shoot an important goal in the semi-final of the European Football Championship at the age of only 16. But to write a book like this, it takes a lot of years in software production and deployment. I have met Bernhard in the middle of the 90s. Since then, we have worked on several software projects together. We have had our share of problems with projects and started to notice the impact of social structures in organizations on successful delivery. After more than 30 years of professional software production and delivery, Bernhard has an excellent understanding of technical requirements as well as the complex social and business settings surrounding software development. Bringing both together is what DevOps is all about, and Bernhard explains it well in this very readable and clear book.

Prof. a. D. Walter Kriha
Distributed Systems and Internet Technologies
Computer Science and Media Faculty, HdM Stuttgart

Preface

For a long time, Software Development has faced the problem of delivering solutions on time and in budget, as well as maintaining and extending the solution within a reasonable timeframe to fix bugs or implement new features. I have experienced quite a few projects which were well financed and staffed and still got canceled because they failed to fulfill the expectations put into them.

The reasons for those failures include long time to market, which was much too long, and poor communication between people in need of some software and those who developed or operated it. Similarly, development and operations were fighting against each other instead of working towards the common goal of delivering results that were worth the money. DevOps emerged on the scene to solve this very problem.

My first serious contact with DevOps was at a workshop about the topic organized by the Java User Group Switzerland. The DevOps novel "The Phoenix Project"—one of the most important books about IT topics in the last 15 years—convinced me, that we need to change the way we deliver software. Agile, while being helpful, just isn't enough.

In my daily work, I often hear people say that DevOps is merely a function and not a transformational task for the entire organization. This was the main motivator to write this book, which tries to convey the idea that DevOps is not about adding another function to your organization, but about transforming the culture of your organization.

It is more about mindset than about special skills and special job descriptions. It's about constantly learning and improving yourself (and of course the whole organization). It's about tying up your bundle and embarking on a journey as a journeyman to learn and improve and ultimately deliver value to the customer.

But wait, there are the voices of sirens whispering to you that it's no longer worth setting off. Artificial Intelligence (AI) has finally reached a state where it will make software developers superfluous. I would like to counter this with a few thoughts on why I think this is not the case.

The threat that some tooling will make developers superfluous comes in cycles of about 10 years. There were program generators. There was graphical programming. There was Model Driven Architecture. You could continue this list with other hypes gone by. Just ask a developer of the new generation if he has heard about those hypes. Very likely, he hasn't.

And now there is a big buzz about AI. It really gets used in development. There are code assistants suggesting you how to implement something. I was watching a demo of such a tool in action, and it was quite sobering. It really promoted bad style! It just filled everything with setters and getters and when you think about it, this was only to be expected.

Of course, such a tool gets trained with the existing large code base and suggests what is common practice. Which isn't necessarily good practice, but practice imitated by many developers. AI suggests the most widespread practice instead of a better way to solve a problem. What will be the result? I am afraid that it will make people believe that what most people do is also the best way. Well, at least it reduces the likelihood of punishment! You rarely get punished for behaving the same way as everybody else.

Another sobering experience was a bug fix I submitted for a software project. I got an email from an AI which suggested lots of stuff I could do to improve on my code submission. Soon after that, my submission was rejected. Maybe we start delegating decisions on what is useful to the judgment of an AI. I am not convinced that AI really understands anything about the deeper semantics. So yes, I want to encourage you to embark on your own journey towards better delivery of better software. In the end, you will likely have a happier and less stressful life working in the software industry. You will probably also need to do less overtime work.

An article in WIRED is very euphoric about the AI-powered future of coding.[1] A simple statistical analysis reveals what this is about. The word "coding" appears four times in the article, the words "programming" and "engineering" only once. Therefore, I think you will profit from AI for coding tasks, but you should probably look to all time masters like Niklaus Wirth when you want to learn about programming or engineering.

Of course, you can do a similar statistical analysis with this book. When you look at the index, you will find that terms like "web shop", "value for the customer", "quality gate", "DevOps", "software delivery pipeline", "acceptance test", "feedback", "transparency" and "trust" stand out. Probably the author thinks those topics are important in the context of this book.

[1] Knight 2024

How to Read this Book

Well, this is not a textbook that attempts to cover a topic exhaustively. It also is not a novel like the excellent book "The Phoenix Project".[2] It is more of a travelogue describing personal travel experiences in the world of software development. The travels lead from being an inexperienced apprentice to a matured journeyman via the stage of ignorance to awareness to reactivity and finally to preparedness.

The first part "Setting the Stage" can be considered as laying out the prerequisites on which the second part builds. You could skip this if you are already familiar with DevOps concepts, but you still might want to read it to refresh the basic vocabulary presented in the first chapter.

The second chapter is about customer orientation. The customer in the context of this book is almost always a medium to large-sized company. There is always a bunch of enterprise applications which need to be integrated. I try to make the topic more interesting by relating some real observations. This is a leitmotif of the whole book: trying not to remain too abstract, but to explain concepts based on specific examples and concrete experiences.

This book will not go deep into all the topics it touches, but provide references to literature you can consult if you want to go deeper. The bibliography is not very extensive, rather a recommendation list of texts that provided more profound insight for me.

* * *

[2] Kim, Behr, and Spafford 2014

The central idea of the second part is to outline how an individual developer can grow from a state of ignorance (regarding the topic of DevOps mindset) to becoming aware of what it takes to deliver better results. From the state of awareness, the developer will learn to better react to requirements and issues and, when reflecting on this experience, to also be prepared for whatever comes his way.

This travelogue is not a blueprint you should strive to imitate! It rather should inspire you to make your own experiences and reflect on them to develop your own proficiency. I believe you can't get there by imitation, but by accepting the challenges that your own professional career offers and by reflecting on them and learning from them. In this way, you can become a journeyman who can judge those challenges on his own and find good solutions for them.

Therefore, I highly recommend structuring your experience according to what makes you aware and how you can react. This mental exercise will help you to be prepared for the challenges of the professional world. In this way, the journeyman is no longer surprised by the adversities of life, which leads to better outcomes.

* * *

Finally, the third part takes an entirely different perspective. Having reached a level of preparedness, we look at the organizational level. There is research which tells us that a DevOps mindset enables an organization to more quickly deliver better software with fewer defects. But research also claims that this mainly works for in-house projects and that this is also related to the cultural type of the organization.

I think this does not necessarily mean that a DevOps mindset won't help you in contractual situations where you do projects for customers. I illustrate this with three example projects roughly corresponding to different cultural types. But I also think that a set of values is important for success, and I begin by describing them to be able to reflect on how those values helped to achieve better outcomes or how their absence contributed to worse outcomes.

This list of values isn't determined by scientific research but just by personal selection. I strongly encourage you to reflect on this in the context of your own experience, and maybe you will find your own set of values that help you develop your project culture.

Part I.

Setting the Stage

1. Three Pillars of DevOps

Before DevOps, the world of software was strictly divided in two: development and operations (of course we can discuss other divisions, like testing and security, but that is not the topic of this book). Development created some piece of software and when it was done, it was thrown over the wall to the operations people. They had to see how they could breathe life into it and keep it alive. This was a very hard job because development did not have much understanding of the needs of operations. The result was often lacking in usefulness and stability. Operations tended to reboot the application servers on a regular basis because they knew from experience that they would degrade over time due to memory leaks and other resource leakages. It was illusionary to imagine highly available software systems. Developers and operators rarely talked to each other, and so the situation did not improve.

But then, clouds appeared on the horizon and the term DevOps became a buzzword. The whole thing caught the attention of the big consultancy operations, who seem to view every technology trend as going through five cycles: innovators, early adopters, early majority, late majority, and laggards. You could also get the impression that you just need to hire some DevOps engineers to be part of the game and thereby adopt a new gold standard. Nothing could be more wrong. But the wrongness is really in the misconception that you could do DevOps by hiring certain skills.

This is a sure recipe for failure. DevOps can't be delegated. DevOps is about the culture of the whole organization. It is about talking to each other and working together across different functions (and not just adding another function and calling it by the fancy name DevOps engineer!). And about taking responsibility for one's work and not ducking away from problems by saying: "This is none of my business." It is about understanding the success of the organization as everyone's business. It's about tearing down the silos enclosing the developers and the operations people, and not about risking the creation of an additional silo for the DevOps engineers and thus making the situation even worse. It is much less about functions and skills and technology adoption cycles and much more about mindset and an attitude to get things done.

I will set the stage by first describing the fundamental pillars of DevOps and about what matters, and then in the second part I will discuss the road for a developer to develop his or her mindset to achieve better results. I won't go too deep into those fundamentals, since there are already other excellent books on this topic. I highly recommend "The Phoenix Project" by Gene Kim, Kevin Behr and George Spafford.[1] This is a very engaging novel about DevOps culture, and it has inspired many successful practitioners. A must-read.

1.1. Flow

The first of the pillars of DevOps is flow. And it really is the first, you can't begin establishing the other pillars unless you have established flow. Flow is the value stream from stating a requirement to delivering it to production. This has to be reproducible and reliable. Therefore, a manual process is not a possible solution, since reproducibility and reliability are just not high enough. Just imagine installing a new feature into production, maybe preparing the production hardware for it, installing necessary dependencies, configuring the system for the new feature, and restarting or reloading affected services. There are just too many steps involved to be able to guarantee that everything has been executed exactly the way it should

[1] Kim, Behr, and Spafford 2014

be. Therefore, all those steps have to be codified in an automatic delivery process.

The same process has to be used to deliver the feature to an acceptance test environment (if you have a separate one) and to all other environments you use for quality assurance such as integration environment, load test environment, or PEN test environment (see section 4.2.5). You always need to get the same results. If something is wrong with your delivery process, everything else takes second priority to fix it. You always need to be able to deliver with your delivery process. The flow must always be in a working condition. If you can't deliver what you produce, you basically produce for the waste bin.

The goal is to create value for the customer, and that can only happen when our work gets released into the production environment. The Scrum methodology has a concept of "definition of done", but much more important is the state "delivered". A definition of done can help us to check certain quality criteria like "documentation is complete and reviewed", "test coverage exceeds 90 %" and so on. But when we exclude "delivered" from our definition of done, then we can fool ourselves into thinking that we are done when in reality, we haven't delivered anything into production, not to speak of producing value for the customer. As long as we are not in production and generating value for our customers, all we do is just work in progress.

The flow of our work packages undergoes distinct stages, and which ones they go through can differ from project to project. We can have a setup where we successively pass the stages of code review, build, unit tests, and acceptance tests on our way to the productive system. Each of those stages constitutes a so-called quality gate, which has to be passed one after the other to qualify our work for production. A more detailed description can be found in section 10.2.

Infrastructure as Code

I want to say a few words about the scope of automation. It is a big step forward from manual software delivery procedures to have an automatic deployment into an environment—our platform—provisioned with an operating system, language run-time, and services like database management systems, caching systems, full-text search engines, load balancers, authentication servers, and so on. As long as this environment is stable and available, we have a high degree of reproducibility, and we can quickly deliver changes with low risk. But what if our platform breaks down or gets compromised? Rebuilding a complex environment can take days to weeks, and in our fast-paced Internet age that is rarely an option.

Taking the idea of automation a step further towards platform and infrastructure eases those concerns. Creating it with automated scripts makes setting up the infrastructure faster and, even more important, reproducible and reliable. As an added extra, we gain the ability to quickly set up variations of our environment or to scale it horizontally.[2] When the version of the full-text search engine is just a variable in our setup script, we can change it and quickly set up an environment where we can test whether the latest version with new desirable features is compatible with our application and also passes e.g., our performance and security tests.

Can we take those ideas even further? Even data centers can break down because of natural catastrophes or terrorism. How fast could we rebuild a data center? We already have the capability to create the walls of a house with a big 3D printer. Maybe one day we can create a whole data center fully automatically. Who knows?[3] You can see that at the level of flow, there are different levels of maturity. The important thing is to get the flow

[2] Vertical scaling signifies choosing more powerful servers and hits a limit, when you use the biggest server money can buy. In contrast, horizontal scaling is achieved by using more stock servers and distribute the load across them.

[3] Google already uses automation to turn up new data centers. See "Software Engineering at Google" by Winters, Manshreck, and Wright 2020, page 523.

started and then continue with the other two pillars of DevOps, feedback and continuous improvement. This will also continually improve your flow.

1.2. Feedback

Flow is a forward-oriented process. But how do we check whether we achieve our ultimate goal of producing "value for the customer"? Here the second pillar of DevOps comes into play. We need to have feedback about what we are doing. There are lots of important feedback loops. Every quality gate[4] has to be passed one after the other and if one gate fails, it is back to square one. We have to resolve the issue and go through all quality gates again since our delivery is now a different one. Each such quality gate is a feedback loop.

Of special importance are the acceptance tests performed by the business people, since they provide feedback on whether we implemented the right thing. Another feedback loop is feedback about our code in production. This is the most important one because this is what will tell us whether we actually achieve "value for the customer". We should actively strive to establish this feedback loop. It will also counter the effect of alienation, which automatically sets in when we aren't concerned with creating value for the customer.

Apart from the value feedback, there is also ample opportunity to gain feedback about our operational costs. We can partially answer resource consumption questions by running load tests, but these tests are always an attempt to model the real usage of our application. The real usage happens in the production system and there we can get relevant insights

[4]When our code progresses from one stage to the next, e.g. from a developer machine to an integration system, it has to pass certain criteria. If those are not met, the so called "quality gate" keeps shut and the code is not allowed to proceed to the next stage which would bring it closer to production. See also section 10.2. Each quality gate represents another set of criteria.

on how much CPU, memory, disc, network, and external services we use. This is also valuable feedback for our work.

Feedback is also an integral part of agile methodologies. Each sprint has a sprint review at the end with the purpose of getting the achieved results accepted by business. Those sprints typically last two weeks in duration, but they can occasionally last anywhere between one week and up to four weeks. This is a big improvement over waterfall type methods where you build the whole application and only then get to the testing phase where you can finally receive feedback from business. This is much too late. I think we want to get feedback even faster than at the end of a sprint interval. The advantage is that our memory of what we did is still fresh, and we are much faster and more efficient in incorporating the feedback.

1.3. Continuous Improvement

After (and only after!) we have established the first two pillars of DevOps, we can and should establish the third one and strive for continuous improvement. It is of utmost importance to have the first two pillars in place first. Otherwise, we can't deliver our improvements in a reliable and quality-controlled way without a well-established flow. Even worse, we can't tell whether we did, in fact, deliver any improvement without having feedback in place that shows we improved some important indicator without making other indicators worse.

It is also important to take small and controlled steps. It is highly unlikely to be able to tell that we improved if we make massive changes. Many of our hard-won indicators will probably be useless if we are rebuilding the world. Modesty is key. Being humble, we will also not claim to have so-called "best practices". This would mean that they cannot be improved, as they are already the best. We should rather strive to execute good practices and understand that we will probably never be done with improving them.

Oftentimes, we want to reinvent the world and put the latest and greatest new technologies to work. Occasionally, this might be an option when we start completely from scratch on a greenfield. But in most cases, there is a legacy, and it is tempting to throw everything away and start from scratch. I strongly advise against this since you would lose the investment already made in the legacy software. You should treat this legacy with respect, since it likely earns money, which in the end pays you. Starting completely fresh means taking a big risk of disrupting this revenue stream. It is better to do piece-by-piece improvement of the structure of the legacy and follow the boy scouts rule of leaving your camping ground in a better condition than it was when you arrived. In this way, you can introduce new technologies into the project but in small and controlled steps.

2. Customer Orientation

2.1. Business Requirements

The DevOps mindset has value for the customer at its core. The customer is the one who has a need for some software and is willing to pay us to develop this software. We need to understand what the customer needs, and this is challenging since normally the customer is not a software expert and cannot articulate the requirements in the form of a software specification. As software developers, we are experts in our domain but not in the business domain.

It is absolutely necessary that we learn enough of the business domain to understand the requirements and to see where they are unclear. We need to ask the right questions to clarify requirements. The clarification does not need to be complete before we start developing. Of course, we need to have enough understanding to start developing, but we need to balance upfront analysis with early delivery.

The concept of a minimum viable product (MVP) is helpful. We focus initially on a subset of the requirements which still constitute a viable product. A viable product is something that already provides value to the customer. It does not realize the full set of requirements, but enough to be utilized, allowing the customer to gain experience with the software product. A concrete product will help the customer to better articulate requirements since there is a reference point that can be referred to.

It is much easier to say that some feature of the product needs to be extended or generalized or that the performance is not satisfying, compared to discussing this on a greenfield where you have nothing you can point at. Of course, this means that we should anticipate that our minimum viable product is not the end of the line, and we need to build it in a way that is easy to modify and to extend.

It may not be a good idea to aim for a perfect specification before we start developing. I think it is important to balance the precision of our analysis with actually delivering something useful on time and on budget and with good quality. Too much perfection can kill your project. Often, a partially effective solution is better than not delivering in a useful time frame. The latter can mean that the project is killed or, in the worst case, that the customer goes bankrupt. On the other hand, when we deliver good value for the money, the customer will ask for more of the same. Producing results is preferable over perfection. This does not mean that we should cut down on quality, but that we need to find the right balance between delivering value and perfect specification.

The three pillars of DevOps are all geared towards achieving the goal of creating value for the customer. Flow minimizes the time we take to deliver a useful work package into production where it can create value. Feedback ensures that we actually meet the requirements with sufficient quality. And continuous improvement helps us to improve the value and the quality of our work.

2.2. System Integration

When we develop enterprise software, our solution will rarely exist in a vacuum. In most cases, it needs to integrate with existing other enterprise systems. We need to have a clear picture of this "landscape" of enterprise systems as far as our system needs to interact with other systems. To get a clear picture, we need to perform a system analysis. As a result, we will have all relevant systems depicted as boxes and data flow between them as arrows (see figure 2.1).

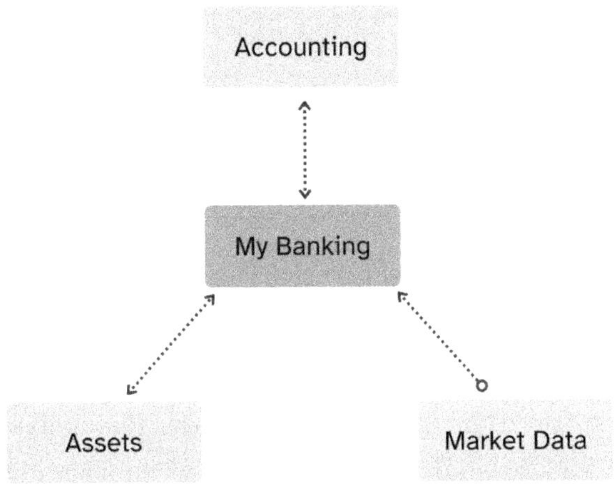

Figure 2.1.: System integration diagram

The good thing is that we do not need to have a bad conscience, putting our system in the middle. The other systems will view the world in a similar self-centered way. Imagine a banking application. It needs to display data from the accounts of the customer, so it will have an incoming arrow from the accounting system. It needs to enable money transfers so it will have an outgoing arrow to the accounting system, as well.

The banking application needs to display the value of the assets of the customer and needs to interact with the asset management system. Besides, the customer should be able to see historic charts and therefore, we also have an incoming arrow from the market data system.

In a next step, we also need to understand the underlying integration technologies and the volume of the data flowing along each integration arrow. We do not want to overload any of our surrounding systems, so we might need to ask them to increase their capacity or to reduce the load by caching often requested data. Other important aspects include who owns which data and who initiated a data flow (push vs. pull). It is

Table 2.1.: Data Flows

Flow	**Direction**	**Owner**	**Volume** (recs/day)	**Freshness**
Account Data	bidirectional	Accounting	5 million	immediate
Asset Data	bidirectional	Assets	1 million	immediate
Market data	unidirectional	Market Data	4 million	1 minute

extremely important to have one system integration diagram to show all those relationships. It is also called system context diagram by IBM.

The system integration diagram is the basis for analyzing the requirements how our software has to be integrated with other enterprise applications of our customer. It allows us to understand how data flows between different applications, which application is the primary owner of some data, and whether data is pushed to other applications or pulled from them. And, finally, what the requirements for freshness and volume of the transferred data are.

I like to put such additional information in an extra table in order to not overload the system integration diagram. To get an idea how such a table can look like, see table 2.1. One important aspect that is missing in such a table is the implementation technology. This will be chosen according to the requirements for the data flow, e.g., volume and freshness. If freshness does not need to be immediate, you can choose asynchronous integration or use caching to improve performance on most usages of the data. When we understand all those aspects, we will get in a position to choose the right technology to solve the data integration requirements. We should not enter this analysis with a prejudice of what the solution will look like. Form follows function.[1]

I want to tell you a short story about just how important such a diagram is. During pre-sales meetings, I like to interactively create such a diagram

[1] "Form follows function" is a design principle stemming mainly from architecture and product design. It was interpreted in a very strict sense by the Bauhaus school of art.

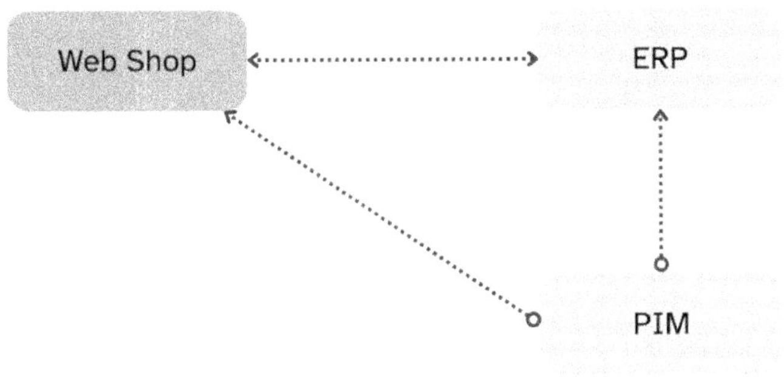

Figure 2.2.: System integration diagram publisher (simple)

on a whiteboard and take this as a basis to analyze the requirements for the data flows needed for system integration. In one such session with a publishing company—which wanted to replace their existing webshop with a more modern one—I had no opportunity to do so almost until the end of the day.

The business people were on the other side of the room and on our side of the room, one of their IT guys was participating who was also not welcome to say much either. Business was chatting the whole day about how to modernize the front-end of their webshop by replacing the underlying technology. I was busy taking notes to grasp the more technical system aspects. Finally, half an hour before the end of the business day our sales representative took a breath and I could chime in, suggesting that we should have at least a brief discussion of the system integration aspects. I offered to draw a system integration diagram of their webshop on the flip chart but was positively surprised that one of the business guys wanted to do it by himself.

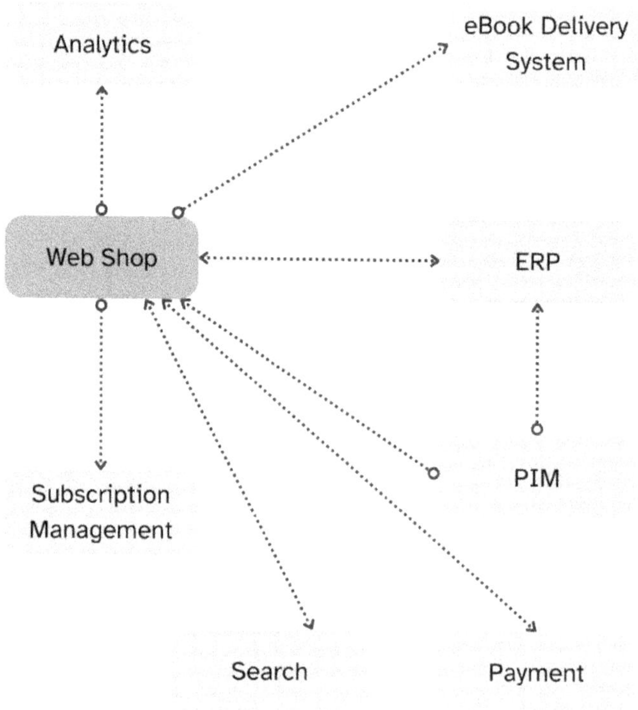

Figure 2.3.: System integration diagram publisher (complex)

He drew three boxes, one for the web shop, one for the product management system (PIM[2]) and one for the enterprise resource planning system (ERP). He also drew the arrows connecting ERP to PIM and web shop and also PIM to web shop, indicating the data flows (see figure 2.2). Then he claimed to be done. I disagreed and said that the diagram was a good starting point, but that I had noted down around half a dozen other systems during the day and whether he would add them to the diagram.

Among them were things like a subscription management system and an eBook delivery system. He did what he was asked to do and once he

[2]Precisely, PIM is the abbreviation for product information management.

connected the data flows, all of them were connected to the web shop, which sat in the middle of all those systems like a spider in its web (see figure 2.3). It became clear from this diagram that the issue was not redesigning their front-end, but replacing this spider in the center of the web and reconnecting all those data flows. Their budget for web design work probably wasn't sufficient to do so.

2.3. Operations Issues

In order to produce value for our customers, our software has to be operated productively. In the early days of computing this was done by people who were called operators and software ran mainly as batch jobs. Later we had interactive systems, and we still needed operators to run our software. This would all work out more or less nicely when our release cycles were long. We would hand over some software to operations, they would install it according to an installation manual and maybe install an update years later.

When software problems arose, the operators usually found ways to deal with them. When they were lucky, the software would issue some error messages that gave a hint to what went wrong. When they were not so lucky, they would have to analyze a so-called core dump or needed to do guess work. Since those days, release cycles have become much shorter. Changes happen on a weekly or daily basis, and in very large systems there can be thousands of changes per day.

It is clear that it is impossible to manually install such frequent changes into production systems. Systems, which consist of many machines, sometimes even of more than one data center across the globe. It is not possible to handle this without automatic software distribution tools. Those tools frequently are owned by the team, which produces the software, but nevertheless there still are specialists who keep the systems up and running.

With increasing demands on performance and reliability, even a new profession arose, Site Reliability Engineering.[3] This discipline systematically deals with up-time requirements by setting up error budgets and won't allow any changes to enter production when the error budget is used up. This follows the experience that most reliability issues stem from changes introduced into the software.

Reducing production changes seems to be in contradiction to keeping up the speed of delivery, but this is only a short-sighted view. When you want to sustain delivery speed, you need to manage some kind of error budget. Otherwise, you run the risk of optimizing for speed only, which will of course work for a short period of time. But over time, the stability of your application will erode, and your delivery speed will more and more converge to zero. You cannot make any changes without introducing more problems and thus eliminate your ability to deliver anything at all.

Of similar importance like the system integration diagram is the system diagram. This shows the internal operational structure of the application, which means all the servers needed to operate the application and how they communicate among each other. Our example shows a load balancer where requests enter the application and which distributes them to the application servers. Those in turn communicate with a database proxy, which manages the communication with a cluster of several database nodes (see figure 2.4).

Between development and operations, there often exists a virtual wall created by the formal structure of the organization. The goal of the DevOps movement is to tear down this wall and to get better collaboration between development and operations. An important aspect of this is that all people involved in the success of a software project should take responsibility. The developer, e.g., should understand what is needed to improve the operability of the software. This starts with simple things like log files.

---

[3] SRE, Beyer et al. 2016

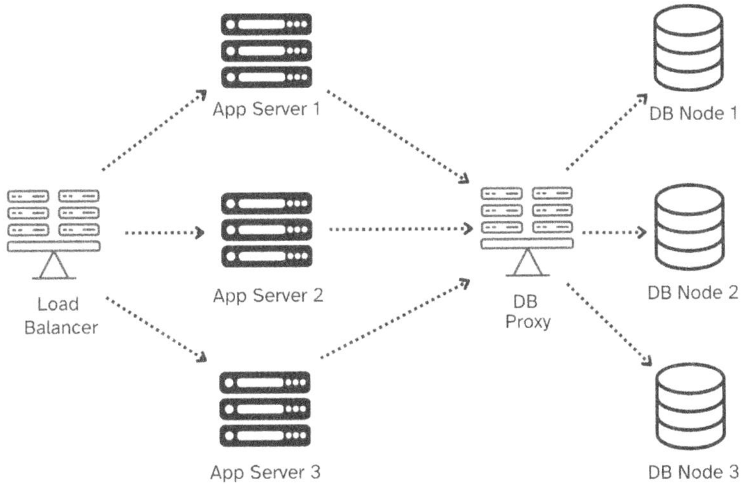

Figure 2.4.: System operation diagram

The messages contained in a log file should be meaningful, and in the case of errors, provide enough context that the error can be understood and fixed. Operations people should not be shy to demand operability designed into the software they have to operate. It can help a lot to go some distance in the other's shoes. It will be eye-opening for a developer to help to deal with operations issues, and it will be fruitful when operations people can participate in the development process (the same goes for service departments etc.).

You have to be wary of Conway's Law ("Any organization that designs a system (defined broadly) will produce a design whose structure is a copy of the organization's communication structure"). This also applies to the separation of development and operations. Operations needs to operate what they get from development, and they will try to defend against getting more of it, raising the bar for accepting changes higher and higher (a completely reasonable approach, given the structural separations).

Adding another function and calling it "DevOps engineers" won't solve the problem but will lead to the creation of a third silo in addition to the silos of development and operation. You can only avoid this trap by understanding it and working against it. Only by transforming the organization in such a way that everybody takes responsibility for the whole can counter this effect.

This book describes two evolutionary paths for this transformation. One for an individual developer who grows from being ignorant of what really matters to being aware, then reactive to issues and finally being prepared for what he might encounter. The other evolutionary path is for organizations, which also can evolve towards a better culture, resulting in better outcomes.

A critical aspect for operating software is that there aren't only happy paths in the execution of our software—although many educational texts suggest so. When they contain example code, you often find the hint "error handling omitted for brevity". But exceptional cases are rarely dealt with. When it comes to robustness in software, it is of utmost importance how it deals with unhappy paths.

Sometimes you see try/catch constructs where the catch block is empty and maybe contains a comment saying "this should never happen". But in the real world, it will happen. Murphy's law ("What can go wrong, will go wrong") applies. If exceptional cases are not dealt with properly, our software will enter an ill-defined state which will make it impossible to reason about what will happen.

Memory leaks often are the most benign result, broken business logic is worse, and it can be very hard to find the source of the issue. Some programming paradigms like Erlang accept that humans are not able to write software that is absolutely correct and follow a "let it crash" philosophy. This means they do not try to fix their state when something is broken, but rather restart the whole failed process. The handling of unhappy paths can be more effort than dealing with the happy case, but when robustness is a necessity, it cannot be avoided.

Part II.

The Road from Apprentice to Journeyman

3. Starting Point: Ignorance

Many readers of this book might have learned the business of software development during some years of training. We have been taught the principles of computer science, stuff like Turing machines and computability, data structures and algorithms, programming languages and paradigms. Maybe we even got some profound knowledge of database theory and probably learned software development methodologies, possibly in an agile way using methods like Scrum or similar.

Equipped this way we landed our first or tenth job as a software developer, keen to use all our productivity enhancing tools like development environments, source code management systems and project management tools to crank out cool software, perfectly architected, elegantly designed and exquisitely coded using all the latest hip stuff on the market. Our company has landed a nice deal for a project with enough budget to pay a team of a dozen professionals for a whole year.

The project is split up into work packages, they are described in sufficient detail to be implemented and prioritized to tackle the necessary and most important ones first. All is nice and dandy, everybody is keen to flex his or her programming muscles. Despite all this, the budget gets used up, and the deliverable is lacking in several aspects. Essential functionality is missing or not behaving as it should. Doing changes is slow and expensive. Performance is abysmally bad.

Our software crashes in unpredictable and hard to analyze ways. How could this happen? We all applied "best practices", followed all the rules in the book of our chosen agile method, used the best tools available and spared no expenses training our team to squeeze the last bit out of them.

There are many reasons why we still fail to achieve "value for the customer". Necessary specialization, focus on technical criteria, training to keep up with the evolution of our programming languages and tools all eat up our available time.

This leads to what we could call alienation. We only see the interfaces of a class we implement. We write unit tests to confirm that they behave according to specification, but we have no concept of the actual value that should be created by our small puzzle piece. We think: "It's none of my business. I am done, when I have committed my feature branch to version control. Others have to take over from there".

As long as we are in this state of ignorance, our results are lacking and often not make it to productive usage. On this level, customer satisfaction is poor or non-existent and likewise, the job satisfaction of the apprentice is not very high.

Example: A Bad Decision Caused by Ignorance

When working at a pretty large software company as a C++ developer, I was tasked with re-evaluating software documentation tools while being between project assignments (and not being billable to the customers of my employer). It had already been decided to use a specific commercial tool, which could pull appropriately tagged comments from the source files of a project and create nicely formatted documentation from it in the form of navigable HTML files.

I think this specific tool had been chosen because it was produced by a commercial supplier, which provided a perception of safety that this tool will be maintained in the years to come. I took a look at this tool from a different angle. I tested it on the project I last worked on, which contained around 150 files of C++ code. The results were sobering. There were about a handful of C++ source files which caused the tool to crash.

I removed or edited those files to be able to generate the documentation for a realistic scenario. The tool took several hours to complete a documentation run. The time needed grew way more than proportionally with the number of input files. The time it needed for a documentation run seemed to grow with the second or third power of the number of input files.

The results weren't even visually pleasing. The navigation icons provided with it were pretty sketchy and seem to have been designed by a software developer and not by a graphic designer. I cross-checked the results with an open-source tool named Doxygen. This one needed no massaging of the input files. It crashed on none of the input files I had available.

It took only a few minutes to document the whole project, and it seemed to scale linearly with the size of the input. The results looked simple but did not hurt the eye. All in all, I could convince my employer to change his decision for a software documentation tool. The first choice was a prime example of how software can fail to meet the needs of users in ways to actually make it utterly useless.

4. First Level: Awareness

We saw in the last chapter how we can fail to create value for the customer. In its simplest form, an application we deliver should be available (it is of no use if it is down); it should perform all the functionalities required to achieve the business goal (Imagine, e.g., a flight booking system. If you can only look up a connection to your destination which consists of several legs, the system is of no use, if you can't book all the legs of your connection together). Beyond functional requirements, there are also non-functional requirements. Our software has to be robust, accountable, fast, and operable with adequate cost and effort.

I know that I can misinterpret requirements and implement something that doesn't fit the customer's needs. I have learned to ask questions when I am not sure that I have understood the requirements in full. I also need to ask questions when I think I understood everything. It is always possible that I understood something in the wrong way, sometimes simply by drawing on the wrong assumptions.

4.1. Wrong Assumptions

Think about an application which has to provide a customer registration so it knows the address where some physical good should be delivered. To accurately calculate delivery costs and sales taxes, we also need to know the region of the address. In the case of the US, those are the federal states like New York or California. Since our first target is North America, we model the regions in a table like the one shown in table 4.1.

Table 4.1.: North American Regions

Region Code	Country	Region Name
NY	USA	New York
CA	USA	California
AB	Canada	Alberta
BC	Canada	British Columbia

The key for this table is the region code and everything works fine since region codes are unique for North America. Our application is in production and delivery costs are always correctly calculated since we have the region code available.

Now comes the day that the business decides to expand to Europe, and to the Nordic countries, Norway, Sweden, and Finland in particular. We see that our previous scheme of using the region code as a key is now a problem, as can be seen in table 4.2. The region code 03 exists both in Norway and in Finland! What should we do? Since our application is already in production, we do not have the freedom to do a greenfield redesign.

We have to do it in a way that doesn't break the existing application, doesn't lose any data we have accumulated so far, and doesn't disrupt operation. If we could do a greenfield redesign, we probably would just extend the region code according to ISO 3166-2 and add the two-letter country code in front. This would turn FI-03 and NO-03 into unique region codes. Since there is too much code in our application relying on the two-letter codes, we follow another route and decide to use the combination of the columns "Region Code" and "Country" as the new primary key. This has minimal impact on our code base, and the necessary schema change in the database can be done without disrupting the operation of our application.

What went wrong here? In our initial implementation, everything worked fine. Should we complain about "changing requirements" or "imprecise specifications"? I think that is not fair. It could well be that there was the

Table 4.2.: Nordics Regions

Region Code	Country	Region Name
03	Norway	Oslo
11	Norway	Rogaland
01	Finland	Ahvenanmaan maakunta
02	Finland	Etelä-Karjala
03	Finland	Etelä-Pohjanmaa

initial view that the application will only be available in North America, and then everything would have been fine forever. It is pointless to think about whether we should have planned for international use.

Nevertheless, we have to accept that business changes in unforeseen ways, and we have to be able to adapt. Sometimes our professional methodologies help (think of core object-oriented principles like encapsulation and separation of concerns) and sometimes they don't. But we always need to consider the context in which we do our work. It is something entirely different to adapt an application which is productive and where downtime is unacceptable compared to a situation where we can afford downtime or even a greenfield redesign.

I think "what has gone wrong" is not the right question. We cannot pin down requirements once and for all, and we cannot articulate them absolutely precisely because we never have full knowledge in advance. The best we can do is to not take our assumptions as absolute truths, but to always question them. We rise to the next level by becoming aware of how we get ourselves into miserable situations.

4.2. Becoming Aware

There are many different possibilities for our software to not achieve "value for the customer". It could be down and therefore not be usable at all. It could be partially available because some of the resources it uses (memory, disk, CPU, external service) are not available or does not meet the expected service level objective (SLO).

It could have functional deficiencies, or it could have non-functional deficiencies, such as not performing fast enough or filling up disk space too fast or saturating the network bandwidth. The way to become aware of all these problems lies in establishing feedback, the second pillar of DevOps. Let's discuss a few ways to do so.

4.2.1. Unit Tests

The basis for unit tests is the idea of a self-contained unit, which has some clear-cut purpose that can be tested in isolation from other units. In the object-oriented paradigm, a unit in most cases corresponds to a class. To my knowledge, the idea has been pioneered by Bertrand Meyer with his programming language Eiffel where he coined the idea of "Design by Contract" and made invariants and pre- and post-conditions first-level citizens of the Eiffel language.

Invariants are conditions that hold for all instances of a class. A precondition has to be fulfilled by the caller of a method and a post-condition has to be guaranteed on return of the call. To illustrate the concept of invariants with a concrete example, let's imagine an address class. ZIP code and city name must always correspond.

A city might have several ZIP codes, but such a ZIP code cannot occur with a different city name. Having separate setters for the two attributes like `setZIP` and `setCity` just won't work, since you can easily break this correspondence. Your API should be such that you—or other users of your

API—can never break an invariant. In this way, an instance of your class can never be in an invalid state.

To have some concrete example in mind, imagine a class implementing the concept of a stack. An invariant would be that the stack always contains at least zero elements. The stack class has methods to push elements on top of if, to pop the top-most element from a non-empty stack and utility methods to test whether the stack is empty and to read the top-most element of a non-empty stack.

A useful unit test suite would test that calling pop on an empty stack throws an `EmptyStackException`, it would test that an initially created stack is empty by calling the `isEmpty` method, and it would test that it can read an element that is pushed on the stack and that it is returned by calling `pop` and also that the stack is empty afterward.

Of course, calling `isEmpty` before calling `pop` won't work in a concurrent context. You need to design your APIs differently when concurrency is involved. You could use a method `popIfNotEmpty` in this context and somehow deal with either getting something or nothing. Anyhow, concurrent access to objects is a thorny topic and if you need to implement locking, it is challenging to get it right, and it will create a load of its own problems. Some modern languages try to evade this by avoiding global state as much as possible and using holding state only locally in a concurrency unit as much as possible. Try to familiarize yourself with Erlang or Elixir or other functional or message passing platforms.[1]

Unit tests provide feedback when we accidentally break the contracts that our unit claims to fulfill. They are a safety net that should always be executed when we change our code base. For this purpose, it is important that our unit test suite executes fast. We should be able to wait for this

[1] When you want to learn more on other programming paradigms, you could read Peter Van Roy's piece "Programming Paradigms for Dummies: What Every Programmer Should Know" (see: Van Roy 2024). There are much more paradigms that just object orientation and functional programming.

feedback to be able to immediately connect it with the cause that probably lies in our last commit so we can immediately fix the issue.

Of special importance is testing the unhappy paths. E.g., think of extending the authentication mechanism of your application. You already have some old-fashioned password-based login and now want to also have some authentication service like OAuth available. For some purposes, you still want to have your old method available. Failing to test not only the "happy path" (user can log in with correct password) but also the "unhappy path" (user can't log in with no or wrong password) can result in suddenly opening your application to the world if you make a stupid mistake when integrating this additional authentication method into your application.

To illustrate how even the biggest players can be bitten by such plunders, I want to show an excerpt from Apple's source code which resulted in a check of SSL/TLS certificates which just accepted any certificate and not only valid ones in listing 4.1.[2] You can see two consecutive identical lines consisting of `goto fail;`. The first one is only executed when the condition above it is true, the other one is executed always. In the end, the function always returns a status signifying no error has happened. For more details, see Adam Langley's Weblog Imperial Violet.[3]

4.2.2. Integration Tests

Non-trivial software systems often interact with other systems to achieve their goals. As an example, an application normally does not implement all the expertise to perform address verification on its own, but instead relies on an external supplier. Such a supplier often provides a web service which accepts an address as input and replies whether it could verify the address together with a regularized version of the address.

[2] Quoted from Apple 2024.
[3] Langley 2024

Listing 4.1: Apple's SSL/TLS Bug

```
static OSStatus
SSLVerifySignedServerKeyExchange(
  SSLContext *ctx,
  bool isRsa,
  SSLBuffer signedParams,
  uint8_t *signature,
  UInt16 signatureLen)
{
     OSStatus        err;
     ...

     if ((err = SSLHashSHA1.update(
         &hashCtx,
         &serverRandom)) != 0)
       goto fail;
     if ((err = SSLHashSHA1.update(
         &hashCtx,
         &signedParams)) != 0)
       goto fail;
       goto fail;
     if ((err = SSLHashSHA1.final(
         &hashCtx,
         &hashOut)) != 0)
       goto fail;
     ...

   fail:
     SSLFreeBuffer(&signedHashes);
     SSLFreeBuffer(&hashCtx);
     return err;
}
```

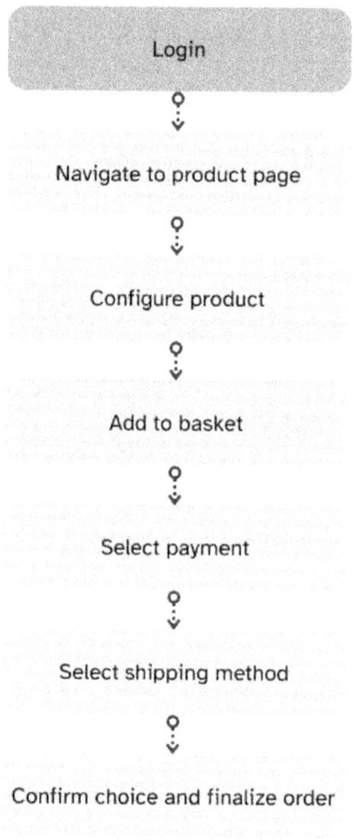

Figure 4.1.: Process diagram

An integration test for such a service would include basic usage of this service by our application. By doing this, we can verify the integration with our application as well as the stability of the external service. We will get early warnings when the external service is not available or changed its behavior in a way that violates our expectations.

Such integration tests are especially important when the services we use are not common "off the shelf" services, but rather "one off" services built by ourselves. In this case, we are the only ones doing quality assurance for those services.

4.2.3. Acceptance Tests

Acceptance tests check whether complete business cases work as they should. For example, in a web shop one such business case would consist of the steps shown in figure 4.1.

Such acceptance tests could be executed manually or by a testing tool which can control the UI of a web browser. Acceptance tests are slow, and therefore you would not integrate a full suite of acceptance tests into your commit test suite. You would want to run them on a regular basis (e.g., hourly or nightly). In this way you won't receive immediate feedback when you commit your changes. Nevertheless, you will get an early notification when you break your business logic without violating your unit or integration tests.

4.2.4. Load Tests

At least as important as the functional tests described above is to check whether non-functional requirements can be met. If the application does not respond in a timely manner or not at all because the web server rejects connections, then it is also not functional. Of course, it is pretty easy to just request a page with a certain number of requests and check how many requests per second are needed to reach unsatisfactory response behavior.

But that is hardly sufficient. A use case consists of a certain path through our application, and it normally also involves a session. Normal operation consists of a mix of several use cases. We have to offer to our application such a mix of typical uses cases to be able to judge whether it is fit for the intended load. There are well established tools that help to generate such loads and that can also provide insights in the form of graphs that show how the responsiveness changes when we vary the load.

It is a good idea to at least regularly run such tests on the staging system.[4] In bigger projects we would build up a dedicated load test system, in even bigger projects we can't really afford to build a staging system that is close to production, and we will use strategies like blue/green deployments (see below) to see how our software changes behave on a subset of our application nodes.

Blue/green deployments are a concept from cloud-native applications. Imagine you have a service running on several containers. The current version running on those containers is called the blue version, and a new release is called the green one. You can put the new release on a subset of your containers and gradually route traffic to the green nodes to see how the new version behaves in production.

If everything is fine and the green nodes can stand the load required from them, you will update the rest of the blue nodes to green. If not, you will roll back the green nodes to blue. This approach usually requires your nodes to be isolated from each other, i.e., they have their own data store. You can also design such an approach with shared data stores, but this is much more challenging since a new release can also contain database schema changes that are incompatible. There still is a way to do such a thing, but you have to be careful to support the old and new schema during such a blue/green mixture.

4.2.5. PEN Tests

Similarly to not being able to serve the required load, an application is also useless if it is not secure. The responsible action to getting aware of a security issue is to take the application offline until we have fixed the issue. Security is a thorny topic, however. There is no way to prove that our

[4] In this book, 'staging system' is used as a synonym for 'acceptance test system'. The term 'staging system' is mostly used in contexts where there are no other quality assurance systems.

application is secure, we can only check whether there is a known way to compromise its security by checking for well known types of security holes.

This is the purpose of penetration tests (aka PEN tests) and it is often done by tasking a specialized company with performing them on a regular basis. It is a good idea to integrate automated PEN tests into our automated test suite to have them executed more often. Some critical tests (e.g., the usage of dynamic SQL vs. prepared statements) can be performed by automatic code analysis.

4.2.6. Monitoring

Monitoring helps us to become aware of whether we meet the availability goals of our application. It is important to be clear about which service level indicators (SLIs) we want to monitor and what the service level objectives (SLOs) for those indicators are. When an SLO is not met, an automatic notification should be triggered, so the issue can be resolved. It is common to monitor infrastructure related SLIs like memory, disk, CPU and network, but we should also monitor platform-specific criteria (usage of thread pools, database connections, caches, ...) and application level criteria (latencies, processing times, failure rates, response times of external services, ...)

I want to tell a story about how monitoring can be helpful beyond the detection of issues. First, I want to stress that it is really a good idea to monitor business relevant SLIs like page load times. I was involved in updating the web shop software in a project to a major new release. The manufacturer claimed that the new release was much faster, but some people in the industry suspected that this was only because the underlying language run-time was also updated to a major new release.

While it is true that the upgraded language run-time offered performance benefits, it was not clear which part of the overall performance gain was due to the language run-time and which part was due to the updated web shop software. It was even possible that the web shop software contributed negatively to the overall performance. Numbers showing the individual contributions of language run-time and web shop software were not available.

In this specific project, we were lucky. A few weeks before the update of the web shop software, we had already cranked up the language run-time, and we also had monitoring in place which measured the TTFB (time to first byte) of a detail page for a specific product. When the upgrade of the web shop software was done, we saw a clear 30 % decrease in this TTFB. Then we knew that the new web shop release contributed significantly to the overall performance improvement.

4.2.7. Logging

The usefulness of logging can't be stressed enough. Who hasn't seen a catch block in an exception handling construct that just contained the comment "this should never happen". Murphy's law dictates that it will happen, and it will do so at the most inconvenient moment. Therefore, the least that has to be done is to log that it happened with as much context information as possible to understand the issue in hindsight.

When you have log levels debug, info, warn and error, the setting for production should be at least info level so you can answer the question 'what happened' by analyzing your log. Of course, it is important to also issue info level log information in your application. For batch processes, this information will at least contain the start and end of a batch process and also information on what has been processed.

It is not sufficient to just have error information. Every so often, we process information and our software does not detect any kind of error, but there is still something going wrong. At least having the information, what has been processed, can guide us in our analysis. Suppressed exceptions are an indicator that the corresponding code was developed under a wrong assumption: that there is only the happy path which needs to be dealt with.

Many textbooks support this view by having comments like 'error handling omitted for lack of space'. Error handling is often omitted in our training. But it is the unhappy paths that need to be dealt with to make a software system robust. Things can and will go wrong in manifold and unanticipated ways. Logging helps us understand failure modes and come up with an implementation to deal with them.

It is important to have useful logging messages that not only make sense for the developer who wrote them. For example, imagine you can't connect to some external service. "Can't connect" is of course better than no hint at all, but it leaves you wondering which service this is all about and why the connection could not be established. Much more useful is something like "Can't connect to REST endpoint for weather service at https://myweather.service, error condition was 'no route to host'".

Sometimes, you are not allowed to log sensitive information due to compliance with legal regulations. You can't log the name of a bank customer, but it might be OK to log the customer type, which might be sufficient to understand the reason for an error condition.

Always log resource use of expensive assets: threads, DB connections, `getResource`, `freeResource` and wait times for getting a resource. This will provide you with hints whether your resource pool is too small or whether the users of the resources hog them for too long. Think carefully before thoughtlessly increasing pool sizes!

4.2.8. Reporting

It goes without saying that business relies extensively on reports for its decision-making. We should do the same for the operational aspects of the software we develop. Having automatic reports at our disposal that tell us per type of request how many have been successful or not and how fast they have been processed helps us to see where stuff needs to be fixed or where there is room for improvement.

4.2.9. Observability

Monitoring and logging are already powerful tools to gain insight into the operation of our software. However, with our software becoming more complex and increasingly distributed, the usefulness of those tools shrinks. We need more insight to understand where requests fail or where processing time is lost. Instrumenting our software so that it reports its internal state to an observation tool is an improvement.

At the minimum, it should contain request IDs and parent IDs to be able to generate nested call graphs from these data. Information about sessions and payloads and the processing state also comes in handy. A good read explaining observability concepts and practice is 'Observability Engineering'.[5]

An easy-to-understand example is queuing at Starbucks. This coffee seller has two queues. One at the cashier where you order your coffee and pay for it, and another queue at the barista who produces the coffee. But how does he know which is your coffee? Simple: He asks for your name and writes it on a cup. This serves as a correlation ID for your order and the corresponding cup of coffee. In this way, you will get the coffee you ordered when it is finally produced.

4.2.10. Business Feedback

Last but not least, it is of utmost importance to have a feedback loop with the business people. They know best what they want to achieve and who their end users are. They should always be aware of what changes we perform on the software system so they are able to connect changed behavior to our changes.

[5] Majors, Fong-Jones, and Miranda 2022

If we are not part of their organization, it is also mandatory that they sign off any changes we bring to the production system because in this case, we have no ownership in the production system but only act as service providers. An important guiding principle is to 'create value for the business'. If we don't, then why pay us for our work?

How do we find out whether we achieve this goal? Feedback from business is one of the most important feedback loops, and at the same time one of the most neglected ones. Maybe this is because we can't formalize it with an automatic test suite and the technical methods of our trade. Nevertheless, there are technical constructs that help us with this feedback loop. During development of a new system, we should make every effort to initialize this feedback loop.

This requires getting up a staging system as soon as possible and to get the flow of our software to this system running by using our deployment pipeline. It also means that we get the integration with the essential surrounding systems working. First and foremost, of course, we need to get the data flow from the upstream systems (i.e., systems we get data from) working, but as soon as that is achieved, the data should also flow to the downstream systems (i.e., systems that get data from us).

To have a concrete example in mind, imagine a web shop. Most of the time, it will need to ingest product catalog data from a product information system (PIM) and it will need to send orders that have been placed to an enterprise resource planning system (ERP) to fulfill those orders. This will let the business do full round-trip testing with realistic data and real data flows. It is important to not fake neither the data nor the data flows. When faking it, you will only postpone the work of getting the real stuff working. And you will risk cheating yourself into thinking that everything is fine while fundamental issues haven't even been tackled yet. By having a close feedback loop with business, we really have a chance to bring our new software system to production.

Everything has been signed off by the business, the load test results give us confidence that we can handle the expected load, and we finally launch the system so it can be accessed by its end customers. Normally, this does not mean the end of our efforts. We might have postponed features to meet the go-live date. Or it might be that new features need to be developed, or that existing features need to be improved or repaired.

We will still use our feedback loop with business to confirm that our changes can go to production. But what about features that take more than about a day to make it from start of development to sign-off for production? A useful construct is feature toggles. With a feature toggle, you can hide a feature in production but have it visible on the staging system.

This way, you can keep up the flow of improvements and fixes while also developing larger features that take weeks or months to finish. Often, it won't be acceptable to stop the world for such a long time. Remember, the first pillar of DevOps is flow, and we need to keep the flow going. When we have a concept of user groups in our application, we can connect the concepts of feature toggles and user groups and have a feature available by simply assigning a user to the relevant user group.

This also gives us more options for operations. We can restrict the availability of a feature that turns out to be overly expensive in terms of resource consumption. By doing so, we keep the whole application going, which would not be possible if an overly expensive feature would bring our application to its knees were it available for every end user. It might even be an opportunity for the business to charge extra for this feature or to make it available only to premium customers.

Using the business feedback loop does not imply that we should rely solely on business for acceptance testing. We should still do our best to understand the business requirements as thoroughly as possible. But we should also be humble enough to recognize that our understanding of the business requirements will be most of the time inferior, and that we therefore need to work together.

Our work is not done once we commit code to the version control system. Actually, our work just truly starts at that point. We need to use business feedback to find out whether our work satisfies the needs of the business. This is partly because the stated requirements can be ambiguous or imprecise, and also because the needs of the business and the stated requirements are not necessarily the same.

As long as our work does not produce value for the business, it is not done but only work in progress. When we commit to version control, we can start to deliver and only then we can get feedback from business and ultimately put our work into production. Then we should strive to close another feedback loop. We should check with business whether we actually achieve value in production.

Often, a business feedback loop is implemented as a weekly jour fixe where the product owner from the customer, the project manager and the lead developer participate. Other service providers will also participate if necessary. This serves as an opportunity to clarify the development status and particularly integration issues with the other services contributing to the project.

In an automotive project with pretty complex business requirements, we established a different format. We had to replace an existing application and therefore needed to provide identical functionalities and additional ones. We were lucky to have access to a power user from the customer twice per week. In this case, we did not send some people higher up in the hierarchy to those meetings, but the whole development team participated and could take turn asking questions to clarify business requirements.

It turned out to be time well spent, since all developers would be on the same level regarding the clarification of business requirements. No matter how business feedback is done, it is of utmost importance that the business people have continuous access to the current state of the implementation so that they can evaluate it. Otherwise, it would be easy to talk past each other because everyone has to rely on the picture in his or her head, and it would be difficult to objectively see where you really stand.

5. Second Level: Reactivity

What should never happen, does someday. Even when we did our best to produce correct, robust, and scalable software, sometimes our efforts fail in one or more of those aspects. And it often does so at inconvenient times. It will happen outside business hours or when the person in the know is on vacation on the other side of the world. When we start producing wrong prices in a webshop, the business might lose more money in an hour than what we earn in a year.

If it crashes, there will be customers looking for more reliable options and the image of the brand will suffer. If we can't handle the number of end users who want to use our application, the result will be similar. In the best case, we will notice an issue before our customer does. Getting notified by the customer isn't the ideal case, but if the customer notices the issue early it is still much better, than issues that go unnoticed for a long time. Just imagine a security hole that gets exploited for an extended time.

5.1. Mitigation

Sometimes, mitigation can be very drastic and consist of taking our application offline until we have fixed the issue. Normally, this is not an option since the business will lose money, customers, and reputation. Hopefully, we have less drastic options available to us. Imagine a full hard drive. This should not happen since (of course!) we have monitoring in place to give us an early warning so we can proactively free disk space or install a bigger hard drive. Still, if it does happen, we can often do a quick mitigation in the same way by freeing disk space or increasing disk space. This will not solve the problem but will buy us time.

What if we can't handle the load of end users who want to use a new feature which turned out to burn more CPU cycles than we thought? If we have a way to switch off the expensive feature or restrict the availability to selected end users, this can buy us time. Scaling up our compute power can also buy us time, but it might not be a long-term solution because it will make our operations too expensive.

Processing a single request can crash because the memory per request is not enough. Increasing the memory per request might buy us time, if there are not too many end users using our software, so we can trade off memory for a reduced number of concurrently executing requests. There are similar mitigation strategies for other resources that we use. On some systems, we need a database connection per request and when requests begin to execute more slowly, the number of database connections in use goes up.

Of course, we might be able to configure our database management system to provide more connections. However, like those other mitigation strategies, this should only be a temporary mitigation until we have a better solution to limit our resource consumption in place. The lesson here is that we can't plan ahead for all possible issues, and we sometimes need to react to them. A good working relationship with operations will pay off in such situations.

I want to relate a story that happened repeatedly in the best intention to improve write throughput of a MySQL database setup. But in reality it was simply a case of activism resulting in harm rather than improving the situation. This should caution you to really understand what is happening before engaging in work based on wild guesses. So let's start.

MySQL supports out of the box asynchronous master/slave replication. In a nutshell, this works by writing all database changes on the master to the so called binlog, which is read by the slave. The slave knows at which position it currently is with replicating and executes the change to its own storage engine. I have observed on several occasions that a project team wanted to take advantage of two database nodes to distribute the write-load on both of them.

In order to ensure that both nodes have the changes done on the other one, they set up master/slave replication also in the other direction, i.e., from slave to master and called this master/master replication (which has nothing in common with synchronous master/master replication btw.). Such a setup is called ring replication in the MySQL literature, and it is not recommended there. It can work for certain applications, but if done naïvely will fail miserably with almost any application not explicitly designed for such a setup.

One example how this can fail is if the application uses a table to manage counters which are used, e.g., to create unique invoice numbers. When you increment such a counter on two database nodes independently, you will, of course, not be able to guarantee that both nodes will not create the same ID and then try to replicate it to the other node. As soon as that happens, it is very likely that a uniqueness constraint in your database schema gets violated.

Be very happy that you have such a schema in place when something like this happens! Otherwise, you wouldn't notice, and your application would happily continue in an inconsistent state. This example hopefully illustrates that normally it won't pay off if you just "do something", even if you somehow hope that it might improve your situation. Normally, you need to thoroughly understand the cause of your pain to find a cure.

Another story about something I would call "activism" goes like this: A colleague was tasked to optimize the performance of a certain request. When he said he was done, I asked him by how much he had improved the performance. His answer really irritated me. He told me that he couldn't tell by how much the performance improved, but that he changed 20 locations in the code where he just "knew" that they were programmed inefficiently.

I find this quite remarkable. Since there was no analysis of the cause of the performance problem, it could not be said that the issue had been resolved. To add insult to injury, there was quite some risk that the behavior of the request had been changed in some unforeseen manner, since too many code changes had been done at once. If a bug had been introduced this way, it would not be easy to immediately tell which one of the changes caused it.

5.2. Analysis of Issues

If you combine the rough classification of our software system as "working" or "not working" with our knowledge of the cause for the state of "knowing why" and "not knowing why" then there are four possible situations: The best is when stuff works, and we know why. We can relax in this situation. The second-best situation is when stuff does not work, but we do know why. We can be calm because we know what needs to be done to get things working again.

Surprisingly, the third-best situation is when stuff does not work, and we don't know why. We are alert, and we will not rest until we have found the cause of our misery. The fact that things are not working keeps us in the mode of wanting to understand what is up. But by far the worst situation is when stuff works, and we don't understand why (see figure 5.1). If we are inexperienced, we might not be alarmed because we think we are lucky. But things that work by chance always break at the most inconvenient moment.

This will probably be during the night or during our vacation hiking in a place far away. We should be very respectful of this situation and do our best to keep it from happening by building comprehensibility and observability into everything we do. We want to make the task of analyzing unexpected situations as smooth as we can, and also make it possible for

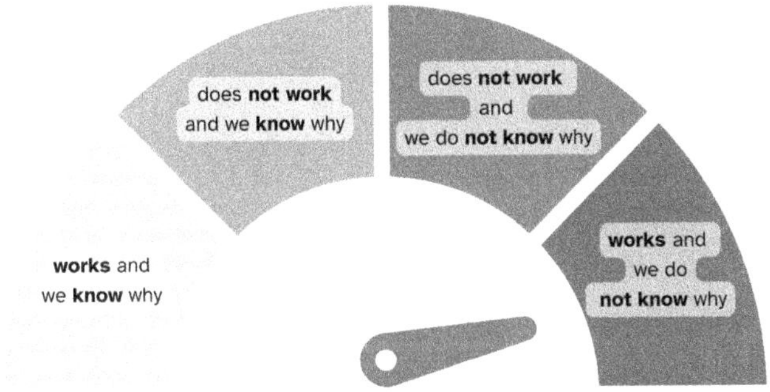

Figure 5.1.: The State of Affairs

others to perform them when we are not available to debug our tangled mess.

So what methods do we have to understand the operation of our masterpiece? On a good day, business is only affected marginally by a problem and can operate with only small restrictions or with a workaround. The issue is well described (a statement 'it does not work' does not count!) and we can easily reproduce it on our development machine.

We can fire up our debugger and leisurely analyze the state of our application and in many cases quickly understand what caused the issue. We fix it and roll it out through our delivery pipeline, which of course has some new automatic tests guarding against the issue we just fixed. Those tests are called "regression tests" since they give us assurance that the issue does not return, e.g., by some well-meaning colleague removing the fix again because it makes the code look so much more complicated.

Apart from the new regression tests, there are also all those other tests in place which test for the contracts of our classes and functions and also prevent other regressions. Business will also perform their acceptance tests, and the world probably will be a better place after we rolled out our fix to production.

However, on a not so good day, the world may not be as well-meaning. Business might be affected substantially, and we first need to find a way to get operations to a partially working state.

Think of some resource being used at capacity, like a hard disk so full that no more files can be opened. We might be able to free up space by removing files we do not need any more. If we are not so lucky, we might need to sacrifice something of lower value, to protect the more important stuff. If the disk keeps filling up again faster than we can remove files manually, we might need to whip up a job that continually frees up space so we can ensure operation until we come up with a real fix.

We also might not be lucky enough to reproduce the issue on our development machine. There can be many reasons for this. It could happen because the production environment is different from our development environment. It might be because the productive data is different from our test data. It might be because the real load is different from what we can simulate on our development machine. Whatever the reason, in some situations, we need to analyze the issue in the production environment.

Some tools that can help us with this task include logging, monitoring and more advanced observability tools, like profiling and tracing. Typically, those tools have a hefty performance impact, so we want to trigger them only on specific application requests initiated by us but not those initiated by the users of our application. Those tools might tell us that we have a performance problem, but it is not located in our code. Instead, the slow execution of some database queries causes the requests to be slow.

We might also find those slow queries with database oriented tooling. Sometimes there is an easy fix like adding an index to prevent a full table scan—which never caused any issue with our small set of test data.

Sometimes it is more intricate. The message here is that we need those tools to pin down the location of the issue and avoid doing random searches. We need to reduce the problem to a size that will fit into our head, while at the same time avoid working with wrong assumptions.

5.2.1. Log File Analysis

I already mentioned how to put log files to use in the chapter about *Becoming Aware*. I recommended to always log when a batch job starts and when it ends. Of course, we want to log when an error happens. But we also want to log, when we execute a special business rule to "fix" the data we process. An example would be if we import users from a system, where multiple users can share one email address, into a system where the email address has to be unique.

We might replace this shared email address with a set of generated email addresses to make sure that they are unique. It is a good idea to at least write a log entry when we do something like that, together with a hint of why this replacement was done. Of course, we have documented such behavior, but it can save our day when we wonder where some email address comes from and see those hints in our log.

Let's describe a few more examples where logging is helpful. Imagine a resource pool for shared resources in a concurrent environment. Such resources can be parsers (they might be expensive to initialize so you want to reuse them), database connections or execution threads. You will implement a pool if you can't supply an arbitrary number of those resources. As a consequence, you want a client of the pool to be polite and not overuse such a shared resource.

So a resource should be given back to the pool rather quickly. Or given back at all, now that I think of it. Adding logging to the resource management of the pool can help answer whether all clients of the pool really are polite. You will usually see in the log when a client claims a resource and (hopefully) shortly after that the release of the resource. Of course, you need to be able to correlate those log entries correctly. Long hold times can help identify usages of the resource that are problematic. By logging information about the requestor and wait time for resources, you can quickly identify the source of the problem.

Another important example is to log request and response for a web service on log level debug (of course, you also log error information on error level). This information can prove invaluable when analyzing issues with your integration of external web services. I have often encountered the situation where a service provider is unable to tell you what response they sent to a request. Often, there even isn't an understanding of the "wire format" which often is XML or JSON or Protobuf.

It depends on your requirements for human readability, robustness and performance which would be best for you. But having the payload of both request and response (and information on the HTTP headers in the case of REST) is helpful for numerous purposes. For example, it allows you to verify if your request was in line with the expectation of the service or if the response really is what the service provider claims it is. You can also use those payloads to put them in automatic integration tests or to execute the request in a web service test tool.

5.2.2. Profiling

I have already lamented about the ineffectiveness of uninformed performance optimizations. Often, you have a hunch why an implementation is lacking performance. You change the piece of code that you 'know' to be slow and go on with more interesting stuff. But guessing rarely leads to good results. A better approach is to measure when each function is entered and when it is left. There are tools that can instrument your code to register those timings for later analysis.

When your program consists of only two functions, it will immediately tell you which one is eating up the processing time. If the first function takes only one percent of the processing time, it will not pay off to optimize it, even if you spot lots of inefficient implementation in it. You need to focus on the one function that eats up the bulk of the processing time.

In real-world code, the function calls are often deeply nested. In such cases, tools that can graphically display so-called call graphs are very useful to spot where optimizations are called for and which options you have, e.g., to introduce caching or to change the implementation for a better performing one.

With compiled languages, you need to compile in support for profiling. There is no such need for interpreted languages. Profiling support can be added at run time. With highly dynamic languages like Perl, it is possible to implement a profiler with a few lines of code yourself, since you have full access to the symbol table at run-time and can replace a function definition there by mere assignment.

I once did this since information on function level wasn't sufficient, and I needed to record profiling information depending on a parameter which represented the data object the function was called upon. In the simplest scenario, you can add timing output to your log to find out where the critical sections of your code are. You also get early warnings at run-time. The clue is to measure and not to guess.

5.2.3. Query Plan Analysis

Relational Database Management Systems (RDBMS) are, despite some hype about NoSQL products, still at the heart of many of our applications. At the height of the NoSQL hype, you often heard people say that

Listing 5.1: Create user and address tables

```
CREATE TABLE `user` (
  `id` char(32) NOT NULL,
  `name` varchar(255) NOT NULL,
  PRIMARY KEY (`id`)
)

CREATE TABLE `address` (
  `id` char(32) NOT NULL,
  `userid` char(32) NOT NULL,
  PRIMARY KEY (`id`)
)
```

RDBMSs are slow. For many purposes, they aren't. But often, we do experience bad performance in the database layer. This is not inherently because there is an SQL database at work. Mostly, it is because the SQL database is not used correctly.

An SQL database can tell you all the facts which can be derived from its data with a more or less complex query. It uses an optimizer to find a so-called query plan which is best suited to get the desired result with the least consumption of resources like CPU and RAM. The optimizer can achieve this only if the database schema is crafted in a way to support efficient queries and to enable the work of the optimizer. If you do not have a database with such a well-crafted schema with correctly defined data types and indexes, you need to fetch all the needed data into your application memory and perform the necessary logic yourself. Very often, you will not be able to achieve the same level of efficiency and performance like a well-honed database optimizer, which has been developed and tuned for decades to do its job.

id	name
a	user a
b	user b
c	user c
d	user d
e	user e
f	user f
g	user g
h	user h

Table 5.1.: Content of Table User

id	userid
a1	a
a2	a
a3	a
b1	b
b2	b
c1	c
c2	c
c3	c
c4	c

Table 5.2.: Content of Table Address

When consulting a large international operation which had its own set of internally developed applications to support its business, I heard some alarming signals that hinted at a database setup that was far from optimal. The development division discussed upgrading the license of the database product they used so they could operate it with more than 128 GB RAM. There was also the suggestion to use hardware with more CPUs instead of investing in more expensive licenses. Both of those suggestions are strong hints that the database needs to build up full cartesian products[1] and can-

[1] The cartesian product of two tables is a table which contains all rows that are a combination of one row of the first with one row of the second table. If the first table

Listing 5.2: Ill performing SELECT

```
SELECT u.id AS userid, a.id AS addressid
FROM user u
JOIN address a
ON u.id = a.userid
WHERE userid = 'a';
```

not use indexes to only access the needed rows and not process all of them to find the needed entries.

I remember when I was working in the last millennium on a banking application on the data access layer. I was also participating in the meet-ups of the DB2[2] user group every month, and I have to admit that I hardly understood why they were always so riled up when one of their database `SELECT`s resulted in a full table scan. The full table scan is the nemesis of database access, and it means that all rows of a table have to be read to find the ones we are interested in.

Sounds not very performant, right? There was one lady who, in her past, had also worked in the development of the DB2 database management system. She kept telling me that I should learn to use the `EXPLAIN` statement. How right she was! `EXPLAIN` tells you how the database goes about to perform your query, and it can give you quick insight into why a query is not performing well.

I will give the simplest possible example. Think of two tables, one containing users and the other containing addresses for the users as defined in listing 5.1. Those tables are populated with a few data items (see tables 5.1 and 5.2).

has, let's say 1,000 rows and the second one 5,000 rows, then the cartesian product has 5,000,000 rows. You need much more RAM to load such a product into memory!

[2]DB2 is a database management system by IBM.

Listing 5.3: `EXPLAIN` query plan for `SELECT`

```
EXPLAIN
SELECT *
FROM user u
JOIN address a
ON u.id = a.userid
WHERE userid = 'a';
```

userid	addressid
a	a1
a	a2
a	a3

Table 5.3.: Addresses of User 'a'

Now we want to find the addresses of user 'a'. We perform the query from listing 5.2 and (unsurprisingly) get the results in table 5.3.

We probably will not notice that this query actually is not performing well with such a small data-set. However, it will slow down noticeably with a real-world data set. But let's check the query plan by executing the `EXPLAIN` statement shown in listing 5.3 to get the query plan shown in table 5.4.

table	type	possible_keys	key	key_len	ref	rows	Extra
a	ALL	NULL	NULL	NULL	NULL	9	Using where
u	eq_ref	PRIMARY	PRIMARY	128	func	1	Using where; Using index

Table 5.4.: Output of `EXPLAIN`

Oh wow, this is the dreaded full table scan! It has to scan all nine entries in the address table to find the addresses of user 'a'! Why is that so? The query plan tells us that it can't make use of an index to access the address table. So let's put an index on the user id column by executing the statement from listing 5.4.

Listing 5.4: Add missing index

```
ALTER TABLE address ADD KEY userid (userid);
```

Now the query plan looks fine as shown by the query plan from table 5.5. The database engine only needs to scan the three address rows actually needed for the result set.

table	type	possible_keys	key	key_len	ref	rows	Extra
a	ref	userid	userid	96	const	3	Using where; Using index
u	eq_ref	PRIMARY	PRIMARY	128	func	1	Using where; Using index

Table 5.5.: Output of EXPLAIN (optimized)

I strongly recommend that you familiarize yourself with the tools your database management system offers for the analysis of slow queries, like slow query logs, query plans and things like the performance schema.

5.2.4. Memory Profiling

Memory is a resource which often is not treated with due respect. I remember the words of a colleague who told me that we didn't need to worry about memory consumption since we have virtual memory. This is of course far from being true. When you need to swap random access memory to disk and then need to swap in a page that is not present anymore in physical memory, access to this memory is much slower.

Think of a factor of 1,000 or research the exact setup of your hardware (there are different kinds of disks, with different access and transfer timings) or better yet, do your own measurements. Often the reaction to 'out of memory' conditions is to increase the memory limits in your run-time settings. Which is not a good idea for at least two reasons.

First, the time will come when the new limit is not enough. Second, when you consider the memory consumption of the worker processes in a web server, doubling the memory limits means on the other hand that you can only have half the number of your workers and therefore only handle half as many concurrent sessions. Therefore, it is of the utmost importance to limit your memory consumption! In languages where you need to manage memory yourself, like with `malloc` and `free` in C or `new` and `delete` in C++, developers often know that they have to be on the lookout for memory leaks.

In environments with garbage collection, developers often feel safe and tend to think that the garbage collector takes care of all of their memory woes. Sadly, that is not true. Often, you need to cache objects that are expensive to construct and often, this is in the form of a static variable on class level which is nothing else than a global variable. Stuff you put in there tends to stay there indefinitely. Memory profiling in such environments is often not a well-known practice. Still, it will save your day when you are able to use such a tool.

5.3. Blameless Postmortems

If an issue was sufficiently bad, we should consider writing a postmortem about it. Postmortems are well described in Google's excellent book "Site Reliability Engineering"[3] and I recommend reading at least this chapter. You might think this practice makes only sense for large operations like Google, but in my view and experience it also makes sense for much smaller organizations that don't even have a dedicated site reliability team, but nevertheless have a responsibility to guarantee the ongoing operation of their software.

[3] Beyer et al. 2016

It is crucial to avoid finger pointing. We will not write "Joe forgot to handle the case of missing reference data and therefore the import of the customer data wrecked the whole system" but rather formulate only the raw facts without putting blame on any person. In the end, all of us make mistakes and if we have to fear coming forward, we won't deal with them properly, and we will miss an important opportunity for the organization to learn from mistakes.

Of course, we cannot document what caused the issue and how we fixed it during the hot phase when we deal with it. But when the dust settles down, we should document important issues. It pays off to write up a postmortem in a structured way. This includes a timeline of what happened from start to resolution. Each step we take in the analysis and in understanding and fixing should be in this timeline.

We also should include an assessment of the scope of the issue to document how far-reaching the effects were (whole site down, some region down, some or all users affected, which functions affected, steps taken to mitigate the issues until the final resolution and so on). Other important parts are an assessment of what was the root cause (or the root causes) of the issue and how we resolved the issue.

Postmortems are invaluable for sharing knowledge. Often, there are similar issues in other applications that we created, and our colleagues will benefit from such a concentrated write-up of our experience. Once I was able to help a colleague who had to deal with a nasty memory leak in a search indexer by pointing him to a postmortem about exactly the same topic in another project. He was so thankful for the help that he wrote three postmortems on a single day himself to share his own experience. An example postmortem is shown in subsection 5.3.1.

5.3.1. Sample Structure for Blameless Postmortem

Summary

Date	2024-02-15
Author(s)	John, Marion, Jake
Status	Resolved, all actions implemented
Summary	Search index could not be rebuilt in full
Impact	Outdated search results were delivered for four days
Root cause	Several memory leaks in the search indexer
Resolution	Identification and elimination of the identified several memory leaks
Detection	Four days after increasing the size of the product catalog, it was found that a new product did not appear in the search index
Mitigation	The issue could be mitigated by increasing the memory available to the indexer and holding back further increases of the product catalog

Action items

- Guess work did eliminate a few memory leaks, but not significantly
- Introducing a memory profiler into the project helped to identify the relevant leaks
- Monitoring for successful completion of indexing was introduced to get early warning

Lessons learned

What went well log entries pointed to some leakage sources

memory profiler was readily available

What went wrong Cranking up memory did only help with a slightly bigger catalog

Analyzing and fixing the whole issue took very long

Guessing did not work out

Where we got lucky Catalog volume increase could be delayed, which gave us enough time for analysis

Timeline

2024-02-02 10:20 Product catalog size increased

2024-02-02 10:23 Fatal error in log: memory exhausted

2024-02-07 11:31 It was noticed that new products could not be found in the search index

2024-02-07 15:07 Jake found out that the indexer did not run to completion by analyzing the log files and noticing the fatal error from 4 days ago

2024-02-07 16:43 Marion implemented a mitigation by cranking up the memory limit for the indexer. The job now ran to completion, but it was very well understood that this would only be a temporary workaround since it would not uphold with further increases of the product catalog size

2024-02-08 14:11 Betty patched the code to switch off internal caching of products, since it was conjectured that this was responsible for ever-increasing memory consumption. This resulted in an improvement, but the memory was still exhausted with a slightly bigger product catalog

2024-02-09 10:10 Memory profiler was installed into the local development environment.

2024-02-12 15:04 First memory profiles were obtained.

2024-02-12 15:24 There was a memory leak in an external HTTP library which was used to (unnecessarily in the indexing context) fetch product images.

2024-02-12 16:33 The leak caused by the external HTTP library was removed by not using those unnecessary remote calls anymore.

2024-02-12 17:55 Memory behavior was improved once more, but indexing now crashed when processing a product catalog just twice the size. Still no satisfactory solution.

2024-02-14 11:46 Further analysis of the memory profile turned up a map on the level of the product class, which mapped variant product ids to parent product ids. Clearing this cache on every iteration finally stopped memory consumption from increasing without limit.

6. Third Level: Preparedness

When we start to reflect on our experiences in such a way that we are no longer surprised by bad events, we leave the apprentice level behind us. We no longer expect that everything just follows a happy path, but we prepare for the unexpected in our planning, processes, and software.

Considering that DevOps heavily borrowed from the ideas of Lean production, we take a look at a few lesser known of those principles to gain even more inspiration. An important trait of a more professional attitude is the constant reflection about how we can improve our way of working in such a way, that we are not only in a reactive mode anymore. We rather strive to achieve a mode of working, where we are better prepared, not only for bad things we already know will happen sooner or later. But we also like to be in better shape for the "unknown unknowns", i.e., events we do not expect. The journeyman is always alert to recognize an unexpected situation. We look at a few ideas how to be better prepared for whatever may come our way.

6.1. Lean principles

DevOps is based largely on principles gleaned from Lean production, which has been pioneered by Toyota for the manufacturing of cars. In my view, the creation of software is not really related to an industrial production process, but the delivery of software to production is very similar to a production process. Maintenance and operation also have quite a bit in common with production processes.

Agile development methods are focussed on creating software, not so much on delivering it in a way, that minimizes the risk of interference with an application already in production. And in a way, that eases operation to be able to respond to issues and to possibly continue serving the application with reduced capacity or reduced features. Developers may think that this is none of their business, but it actually is.

As soon as we get into the mindset of creating value for our customers, we will understand more and more that we need to create and deliver our software in a way, that is in line with this value proposition.

6.1.1. Andon Cord

The Andon cord is literally a cord which can be pulled by every production's worker to signal problems in production. The effect is to immediately hold production and stop to fix the issue. This is similar to software delivery pipelines. If such a pipeline fails in some way, either because a quality gate cannot be passed or because of some automatic tests are not green, or if the pipeline itself is broken (e.g., because of hardware issues) everything else will take second priority and the pipeline will have to be fixed.

This could mean that all team members focus on fixing the issue before they continue with their regular tasks. In the end, they would not be able to deliver their work if the pipeline is not in a suitable condition to do so. Some teams take the visibility of the pipeline state very serious and use big red and green lights or other high visibility means to signal when the build process is broken.

Occasionally, you see the opposite. The tests executed by the build server have errors, but the team overrides this and merges changes nevertheless to "get things done". Or even worse, they may remove the offending unit tests. When I first heard a colleague say "fake it till you make it", I thought he was joking. I later learned that people mean it nowadays. It goes without saying that the quality deteriorates.

6.1.2. Kanban

The core of this principle is to not produce work units and push them into a buffer, but to pull work units that are actually needed. The time it takes for a work unit to flow through the production system (delivery pipeline in the case of software production) is reduced by 90 %. This is not true in general, but it is in the end a consequence of Little's Law which says

$$\bar{t} = \frac{\overline{items}}{\overline{deliveryrate}}$$

This means that the average time for a work item to be processed is the average number of work items in the queue divided by the average delivery rate. If you remember your overstuffed last Scrum board, you might be able to imagine that it would be possible to limit the work in progress to a tenth. Of course, your mileage may vary.

Reducing the time for work to move through your pipeline is a very important goal to strive for. Not only does business get value out of our work sooner and can sooner pay for our current and future work, but it is also much easier to incorporate any feedback from production, since the work unit is still present in our minds. Of course, we do not want to sacrifice quality and our delivery pipeline ensures that we do everything to achieve the highest possible quality by passing all our quality gates.

There is a saying in the open-source community to "release early, release often". This in essence captures this same spirit, although I don't think it is inspired by Lean production but rather by experience. I believe that there is often room for improvement in this area. Often development is based on feature branches which will be merged into a main branch when ready. This is all fine and good as long as the features are small and make their way through the delivery pipeline in a short time, maybe a day, to be concrete.

But sometimes we work on features that take several days or weeks to develop. Then we get into all kinds of trouble. We might have a hard time merging our work to the main line when we have diverged from it for a longer time. But worse, our work might fail acceptance tests *and will block our delivery pipeline for an unacceptable long time.* One way to deal with it would be to split our work into smaller units that flow more smoothly through the pipeline.

Another way could be to hide our feature with a feature toggle which is deactivated for production (maybe switched on for certain users to be able to test the unfinished feature in production). It is important that the feature has no side effect when it is switched off. A good coverage with automated tests helps to ensure that. When our feature development is complete and acceptance tests are positive, we might remove the feature toggle from the code.

6.1.3. Poka Yoke

Poka Yoke means the avoidance of unintentional errors. This has a significant impact on many aspects of software production, ranging from design over implementation to delivery. Error avoidance is a premium way to prepare for smooth production. Or as Sun Tzu says in his famous book "The Art of War": "The greatest victory is that which requires no battle." This cannot be stressed enough.

If you avoid errors, you do not need to deal with them, you do not have expensive downtimes because of them, you do not have sleepless nights trying to understand what went wrong and how to fix it. Keeping things simple is helpful to avoid errors, but not sufficient. Type safety is a basal way in programming language to prevent using data of the wrong type, which could lead to all kinds of unexpected behavior.

Using framework principles can make your software much more robust by guaranteeing expectable behavior. Good industrial design can be a big inspiration for software design. For example, a good design for plugs and sockets does not just use some color marks to indicate how the two have to be connected, but will use geometrical constraints to prevent wrong connections (see figure 6.3).

In software delivery, a well-maintained delivery pipeline goes a long way towards preventing errors. Therefore, we should always make it a top priority to have good coverage with automated tests and immediately react when the pipeline is red. We should also keep our delivery pipeline fast (this partly contradicts the requirement of good coverage) so we have to make our tests fast and make wise choices what needs to be executed to give a green light for passing to the next stage.

6.1.4. Kaizen

Kaizen roughly translates as "change for the better". This relates directly to the third pillar of DevOps, but has a broader scope. The Japanese term more accurately is interpreted as continuously questioning your assumptions for the well-being of your customer to reach a solution that is best for all parties involved. In short, you could phrase it as "always check your assumptions". Kaizen encompasses much more than continuous improvement to our software or our delivery process. It also refers to continuous education of the coworkers, suggestions for improvement by the workforce, and leadership which is oriented towards the workforce.

6.1.5. Muda

Muda refers to the elimination of waste. Waste is every activity or artifact which adds no value. In a software context, that could mean too much code. The holy grail is the reuse of code, which can happen on several levels. Copy/paste reuse usually isn't reusing but creation of waste. Copied code can diverge and therefore will do so. Sometimes, it is argued that we need to adapt code, but if we do this by copying and modifying this is normally a sign of bad design.

Re-executing tests in a delivery pipeline when it is guaranteed that we get no other results is waste, which slows us down. A famous saying (probably wrongly) attributed to Albert Einstein is "Insanity is doing the same thing over and over again and expecting different results". For instance, it doesn't make sense to do automatic style checks on code that has already passed.

This should only be performed on new or changed code. We also should not put generated artifacts into our repository, but instead generate those artifacts. In order to speed up our pipeline, we can use caching, but we should not add waste to our repository. Manual execution of repeating steps is also waste that should be automated and left to the machine, which is not only more reliable in executing tedious tasks but usually also faster.

You might want to argue that, e.g., microservices architectures violate the principle of waste elimination. In such an architecture, you deliberately have several copies of the same code in different services. You might need to port new features or bug fixes to those other services, which is of course a kind of waste.

But still, also those architectures strive to minimize waste, although of a different kind. The kind of waste you avoid in this case is friction loss resulting from tight coupling. If your organization is big enough (think of thousands of developers working on the same project), tight coupling of your services can slow you down so much that you completely lose your ability to deliver something in a reasonable amount of time.

6.2. Putting it to Work

> "The computer is based on the same simple principles as sixty years ago. But performance has increased millions of times over. However, the effect of this increase in performance on programming is very negative—especially on the discipline of programming. In the past, resources were extremely limited, whereas today everything is available in vast quantities: Memory, computing power, transmission capacities, simply everything.
>
> Nobody has to save anymore. Programming, however, means maintaining discipline and taking care at all times to avoid unnecessary complexity. This way of thinking is disappearing more and more. Because such optimization takes time. It would be much more expensive than simply buying a bit more hardware. That's why it's not being done."
>
> Niklaus Wirth (February 15, 1934 – January 1. 2024) in an interview with Technology Review in 2016

We have examined what the three pillars of DevOps are, and we also have looked at Lean principles that inspired the DevOps movement. We think that those principles still can inspire us to improve our work and our ultimate goal to deliver value for the customer. This also means to deliver inside temporal and budgetary constraints, and to be able to remain capable of delivering improvements and changes within tight constraints.

It is no good if we can deliver a minimum viable product (MVP) on time and in budget, and then need the same money and time to make small changes. We must be able to grow our work in a steady way. Let's see how we can prepare ourselves to be able to do so.

6.2.1. Limit Work in Progress

To establish a good Flow in your delivery pipeline, it is important to limit the amount of work in progress. This follows from Kanban. In extreme cases, failing to do so can clog your pipeline in a multitude of ways. If you do not respect the Kanban ideals, you will continue to push stuff into your pipeline even if your automated tests are red.

More and more effort is required to fix your software so that the tests pass (not the other way round! You should not fix your tests if they are well-designed). This will slow you down and severely hamper your ability to deliver. If you require a sign-off from business to finally push your changes to production, it is also a big advantage if the amount of work that must be signed-off is strictly limited.

A good rule of thumb is to be able to have a high-level overview without needing notes. Having too many work units will require significant effort from business to check the integrity of your application. It gets even worse if you continue to add changes that need a sign-off. To limit damage, you might want to call out a feature freeze to unclog your pipeline.

This means not putting additional units of work into the delivery pipeline until it has been unclogged. Failing to limit work in progress can result in pipelines being clogged for months. This violates our ultimate goal of providing value to the customer.

6.2.2. Follow the Boy Scouts Rule

The boy scouts have a rule that says, "Always leave the campground cleaner than you found it." This is an excellent rule which shows respect for your colleague who has to maintain your code in the future. Often, you are this colleague yourself. You will be glad if you restructured your code in such a way that it is more readable and easier to understand.

This goes a long way towards being able to fix or extend it. One important aspect is to have clean code. This means well-formatted code following clear conventions, using well-known design patterns, not writing obfuscated code but preferring clear structure over overly clever or "cute" solutions.

It also means refactoring your code towards better design. The ideas have been pioneered in the book "Clean Code".[1] User experience is not just for end users, but always consider that your code also has users who will be thankful for a good user experience. This does not go only for clean code, but also for good interfaces that are well-designed to make them easy to use and hard to misuse.

6.2.3. Avoid Coolness

I can't repeat this often enough: *Cool is not a substitute criterion for useful.* There is a big problem when developers do not have sufficient understanding of the business needs. When this is the case, we would rather strive to make our solution "cool" than useful because there has to be a success criterion, right? And in the absence of an external success criterion, we make up our own.

Often it's even worse. We have a new thingamajig, and it has to be the perfect match for the task currently assigned to us. The cool kids on the block also use it, and they are really so cool, and we also want to be like them. Very quickly, we will use a new library or a new component because we heard it supposedly performed miracles in some context that isn't even vaguely similar to our own situation.

The danger is that our evaluation criterion is just coolness. But this should never be accepted as an evaluation criterion. Important (and business relevant!) criteria include performance, robustness, operability, repairability and extensibility. If it is challenging to analyze issues occurring

[1] Martin 2009

in operations, how should you come up with a timely fix? When something does not work, you want to very quickly be able to reproduce the problem with your debugger, allowing you to examine the internal state of some code.

But when you are under time pressure, how quickly do you find out how to get a debugging session going on some processes started by some middleware? Maybe that middleware is a real benefit for your project. In that case, you need to go "all in" and understand it inside out. This includes being able to debug the decisions of the middleware, being able to debug processes controlled by the middleware, knowing how to operate it reliably and securely.

That is quite a lot and may take years to master. So you might be better off not going for the cool stuff but staying with what you are familiar with. Don't search a problem for your solution. That's not good engineering practice. Good engineering practice strives to find the appropriate solution for a problem and not the other way round. Which of course also means that you need to master more and more solutions over time.

6.2.4. Avoid Complexity

We will look at some real examples of how overly complex solutions can seriously hamper the working of your software, and see some of the bad consequences that stem from hubris when choosing to implement more complexity than needed. It's like the sorcerer's apprentice who tries to conjure some magic in the absence of the master and completely loses control because he doesn't know how to control this power.

Complexity hinders comprehensibility. Do not make your designs more complicated than necessary. Avoid unneeded complexity if there is no good operational or business reason for introducing it. For example, do not introduce abstract classes or interfaces if there will ever be only one class inheriting from it or one class implementing the interface.

Do not justify such a design by saying it might come in handy in the future. *Cross this bridge when you get there.* It is easy extracting abstract classes or interfaces with modern IDEs. And when you get there, you will have a much better understanding of how those abstractions actually should look like.

Do not implement multi-pass processing when there is no good reason for it. I have to maintain a data import construct which does exactly that. It first transforms external data into an internal XML format, which is then processed by a second step. Experience shows that it is much harder fixing or extending such a design. It often takes hours or days to reproduce and localize an issue instead of minutes when you have a direct one-pass design.

Another disadvantage is that it will rarely have a good performance and that latencies for processing are bad and difficult to predict. There are good intentions behind such designs, like reusing the processing implementation of the internal format. The benefits rarely outweigh the downsides. Therefore, you should always also consider the downsides of your design decisions and resist if there is no clear advantage.

Reducing complexity will always help to fix and extend your software in the future. If at a later point you need more complexity, you will know what you need, and then you should refactor to add this needed complexity. Do not introduce message queues just because they are cool. Have a clear understanding of at least basic queuing principles to not create havoc of byzantine dimensions.

I do not want to say that there is no place for message queues. Sometimes they will save the day. But in some instances they will really hamper your system. I will discuss two issues that can really harm you. In one case, a message queue was used to synchronize the category tree between a web shop and a content management system, which was used for marketing content in the shop.

Figure 6.1.: Overflowing Message Queue

After running for a while, it was noted that the queue had more than a million entries (illustrated by figure 6.1). Upon measuring the processing time needed for one message on the receiving end revealed that it took at least a second to be processed. A quick calculation strongly suggests that it would take at least 11 days to empty the queue. Defending such a design by saying that it will be "eventually consistent" sounds like utter mockery to me.

In 11 days it is very likely that the data at the source have changed again and so the state of the total system will just never be consistent. Of course, you could try to improve the situation by adding more workers on the receiving side, but this will add more complexity, and you might not be able to do it at all because your receiving end just cannot cope with parallelization.

Figure 6.2.: Professor Butts and the Self-Operating Napkin by Rube Goldberg (1933)

It also might be just too expensive. If you want to improve your processing by a factor of 10, you need around 10 times as many resources for your workers, and it might be too expensive to operate it. You also need better qualified software engineers to get it working and to operate it. Little's Law discussed in the section about Kanban of course also applies to software queues.

In another case, a queuing solution for a data import component turned out to be underachieving in performance (5,000 records per hour compared to 200,000 records per hour achieved by a much simpler and more modest design). Furthermore, it did not operate in a robust way. For one, it used data processing workers that were unable to re-establish a lost database connection. This required a restart of the entire "Rube Goldberg machine".[2]

[2]Everybody has seen a video of a "Rube Goldberg Machine". It's a complicated apparatus executing one nonsensical step after the other for no apparent purpose other than being complicated and extremely difficult to calibrate that all the intended steps are actually executed. The term goes back to the American cartoonist Rube Goldberg who loved drawing such apparatuses like his self-operating napkin (figure 6.2). The

The smaller issue was that the messages did not actually contain reasonable transaction units which caused massive consistency issues in the target database. I think it's often a good idea to stay away from the complexity of queues. Particularly, if they are not a natural fit for your implementation platform and there is no compelling reason to make your system more complex than it needs to be.

It also pays off to think through your queuing design with easy to grasp analogies like the dishwasher problem. The dishwasher puts the cleaned dishes on the rack and the dryer picks them up to dry them. You will easily be able to imagine a lot of issues with this elementary queuing construct. When the dishwasher is faster than the dryer, the rack will fill and the latency will get worse and worse.

When the dryer picks up the last dish first (last in first out), the latency for the first dishes will be infinite. If he goes first in, first out, the time for a dish to get dried grows and grows. Enter parallelization. Senders and receivers need to be coordinated, and they also need to be paid. There is no such thing as a free dishwasher or a free dish dryer or even a free rack.

Understand if the complexity you want to introduce into your system is just Muda and resist when you notice that you just will create unneeded waste. Your operations will get more difficult by adding complexity.

6.2.5. Avoid Flexibility

We often have encountered advocacy for flexibility, or even done so ourselves. I make the case for the opposite. Avoid flexibility when it is not needed. Well-intended flexibility can result in bugs, which are hard to hunt down and fix for good.

---

term is also used to classify designs that seem to strive for complexity for its own sake. Sometimes such a machine does have a purpose, but the means to achieve it go way over the top.

Flexibility lies in the opposite direction of robustness. I want to illustrate this with a real-world example. Many applications require a search service, and the index of this search service needs to be updated when the application data change. The code doing this update should work robustly and reliably.

A typical anti-pattern ...

I present an example how such an integration failed to achieve this goal. The application in question had to serve its content in about 20 different languages. The behavior of the indexing code was strange, it resulted in German texts ending up in the English language index, although the indexing logic apparently sets the language correctly.

An essential part of the code is the class `Indexer`, shown in reduced form in listing 6.1 in pseudocode. This pretty class does a few more things (maybe not a clear "Separation of Concerns"?), but it is used as shown in listing 6.2.

This looks reasonable at first glance, especially when it is embedded in a larger code base. The problem is, however, that `Indexer` has two member variables `langId` and `langIsoCode`, which should be constrained (the ID must always match the ISO code). However, this constraint does not exist in the code, but at best in the developer's head, and is not enforced by the construction of this class.

... and the problems that arise from it

The problems already start in the construction phase, which allows the creation of a dysfunctional object. The public setters and getters allow any external changes that may violate the connection between the ID and the ISO code. These issues persist throughout the life cycle of the object:

Listing 6.1: Flawed search indexer

```
class Indexer
{
  private int langId = 0;
  private string langIsoCode = null;

  public Indexer()
  {
  }

  public setLanguageId(int id)
  {
    this.langId = id;
  }

  public int getLanguageId()
  {
    return this.langId;
  }

  public setLanguageIsoCode(String isoCode)
  {
    this.langIsoCode = isoCode;
  }

  public String getLanguageIsoCode()
  {
    return this.langIsoCode;
  }

  public index(String key)
  {
    String view = Database.getLanguageViewFor(this.langId);
    String value = Database.readFromView(view, key);
    this.sendToIndex(key, value);
  }

  private sendToIndex(key, value)
  {
    // write value at key into search index
  }
}
```

Listing 6.2: Usage of flawed search indexer

```
String keyToIndex = 'myKey';
Indexer indexer = new Indexer();

foreach (Languages: String langIsoCode) {
  indexer.setLanguageIsoCode(langIsoCode);
  indexer.index(keyToIndex);
}
```

The user must be very careful to always set both arguments to match beforehand. So this class also has a big usability problem.

It would be best to create Indexer as an immutable class,[3] which takes only either the ID or the ISO code of the language as constructor parameters and thus can only be set correctly and can no longer be put into an incorrect state by calling a mutating method.

If the class really has to be mutable (which can often be avoided), then there should be no mutation that creates an invalid state. Imagine a setter for either the ID and the ISO code, or a setter that takes both as parameters and can recognize an incorrect combination of the two parameters.

Cross test: Does the pattern score with flexibility?

But how often has a design such as the above been defended by a programmer as desirable because it is "flexible"? After all, in many books (which perhaps should never have been printed) exactly a style like this is shown. Since I can no longer count the number of bugs that can be traced back to this anti-pattern, I call it "challenging fate".

The beloved "flexibility" all too often leads to an instance of such a class being placed in an invalid state and the connection between cause and effect is often not easy to recognize, since both are far apart in the code base. On

[3]For an implementation of an immutable `Indexer` see listing 6.3.

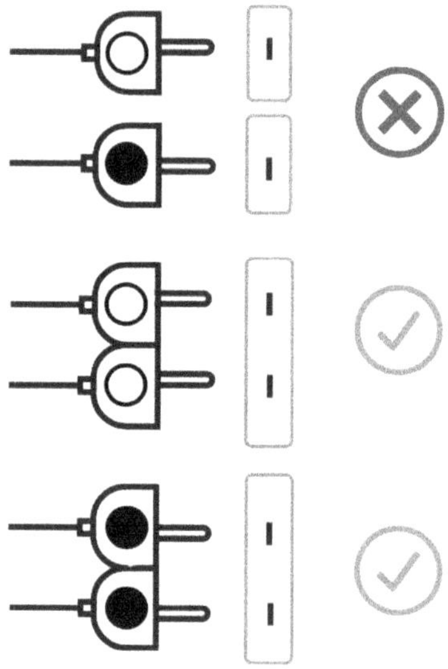

Figure 6.3.: Flexibility as Source of Errors

closer inspection, the described anti-pattern does not make the code more flexible—e.g., by interfaces and polymorphism—but simply introduces non-determinisms.

The inversion-of-control or Hollywood principle ("don't call us, we call you"), on the other hand, contributes much more to the robustness of software. In the object-oriented world this can be found in frameworks or in the form of the "template method" pattern, in the functional world it can be found in Erlang/OTP as so-called Behaviors.

The reason why this design technique leads to robust code is simple: Here, reuse is performed in the best DRY manner (don't repeat yourself) and the errors in a framework (or Behavior) are reduced by every concrete realization of the framework. A pleasant side effect is that the behavior of software based on such principles is more predictable and shows no unexpected behavior. This way, the developer stays in control and no longer challenges fate.

Flexibility vs. Robustness

The interesting thing is that robust programming techniques have been around for a long time and that they are still used successfully in modern software ecosystems. Nevertheless, bad practices are still widespread and therefore difficult to eradicate. It seems like you need to experience it yourself that life as a software developer is not made easier by "flexible" designs, but rather by robust ones.

This is because the main work effort is not in the quick creation of a "proof of concept". Instead, it lies in the so-called maintenance phase, in which bugs have to be corrected, and new requirements implemented in such a way that they do not introduce any new bugs. Avoiding unneeded flexibility for the sake of robustness is an application of the idea of Poka Yoke. You avoid stupid mistakes by eliminating the design causes for them (figure 6.3).

Immutable Version of the Indexer

For completeness's sake, I also want to show the code for an immutable `Indexer` (see listing 6.3). When you look at this code, you will see that there is no way to confuse an instance of the class `ImmutableIndexer`, since it only has `langIsoCode` in its state. It is also not possible to change such an instance during it's lifetime, since it has no setters and therefore can't be changed.

So it offers much fewer possibilities to create havoc than the version discussed previously. Of course, its usage also differs a bit. We have to create such an `Indexer` for every language. If we need it more than once,

Listing 6.3: Immutable search indexer

```
class ImmutableIndexer
{
  private static Map<String, int> isoCodeMap
    = Map.of("de", 1, "en", 2, "fr", 3);

  private String langIsoCode = null;

  public Indexer(String langIsoCode)
  {
    this.langIsoCode = langIsoCode;
  }

  public index(String key)
  {
    String view =
       Database.getLanguageViewFor(this.getLanguageId());
    String value = Database.readFromView(view, key);

    this.sendToIndex(key, value);
  }

  private int getLanguageId()
  {
    return isoCodeMap.get(this.langIsoCode);
  }

  private sendToIndex(key, value)
  {
    // write value at key into search index
  }
}
```

we will want to create a registry where we keep those instances and can look them up via the language ISO code.

Listing 6.4 shows a code example of how to use the immutable indexer.

6.2.6. Make APIs Hard to Misuse

APIs (application programming interfaces) are user interfaces for developers. There is a lot of talk about user experience (abbreviated UX) and this is normally in the context of end user interfaces which are often graphical user interfaces. UX is about ease of use, about simplicity, about fun and

Listing 6.4: Usage of the immutable search indexer

```
String keyToIndex = 'myKey';

foreach (Languages: String langIsoCode) {
  ImmutableIndexer indexer = new Indexer(langIsoCode);
  indexer.index(keyToIndex);
}
```

about achieving a purpose with some software. But what about the user experience of a developer using an API?

This could be a library of functions, some class, or a collection of classes, or a remote service. Basically, the same principles that hold for the design of good (end) user interfaces also hold for the design of programmer interfaces. They should be simple, intuitive to use and hard to misuse. And they should be there to achieve a purpose. Of course, you can write whole books on the topic of API design, so this section cannot possibly be exhaustive. But I try to list a few important principles that should make your life and the life of the users of your code easier.

Purpose

Stick to a well-defined purpose that doesn't require guesswork how to use your API. Use natural usage pattern instead of cute ones. Namespaces like "util" or "misc" are more often than not a collection of classes or function for which the designer did not know where to put them. The user of your library has to look into this bag of stuff to see if there is something useful in it. Often, it does not fit quite right, so it has to be adapted anyhow.

Simplicity

"Make things as simple as possible, but not simpler" is a saying attributed to Albert Einstein. It's an important guideline, and it expresses that you

Listing 6.5: DataTransfer class

```
class DataTransfer
{
    public DataTransfer(String connection);
    public bool isNetworkCardPresent();
    public bool isInternetAvailable();
    public bool isFirewallOpen();
    public transferData(String payload);
    public void tearDown();
}
```

need judgment and experience to tell when something is simple enough and should not be made any simpler. An example would be the modeling of a business domain. You will express business concepts with classes or perhaps data structures.

A good example is the combined plug example of the last section. By only allowing both needed values to be passed together, you achieve simplification and in this way avoid possible misuses. Another example would be a class for addresses. It could contain interfaces that have nothing to do with the concept of an address, like some method `getInhabitants`. Leaving such methods out makes the design simpler and more versatile.

There could also be methods to retrieve associated contracts, like rent contracts associated with this address. Again, such things should not be there. In the opposite direction, you could make your model too complicated by being too granular. Most of the time, you should not model concepts like city, street, and house number with dedicated classes. It makes sense to have type aliases for such concepts to gain some type safety, but most of the time, your budget is spent better implementing useful stuff.

A more important consideration could be which types of addresses you need to represent. Some addresses do not have street names and house numbers but house names! Unnecessary protocols can also make your life harder than necessary. Imagine a class facilitating data transfers. It might

Listing 6.6: Usage of the DataTransfer class

```
DataTransfer dataTransfer =
    new DataTransfer(connection);
if (dataTransfer.isNetworkCardPresent()) {
    if (dataTransfer.isInternetAvailable()) {
        if (dataTransfer.isFirewallOpen()) {
            dataTransfer.transferData(payload);
        } else {
            // inform user that firewall is not open
        }
    } else {
        // inform user that Internet is not available
    }
} else {
    // inform user that there is no network card
}
dataTransfer.tearDown();
```

be necessary to have methods to open and close a connection to be able to properly handle common failures in those steps.

It would be overkill to add methods to check for the presence of a network card, to check for the presence of an Internet connection and to check whether a firewall is open to be able to do the data transfer. Listing 6.5 shows a class with such a design. Listing 6.6 shows how such an abomination would be used.

Of course, this example is intentionally contrived, but it shows that APIs that require you to keep to a certain protocol (execute all those tests in the given example in the right sequence and react appropriately) are hard to use right and the code that uses them is hard to read and maintain.

Of course, we know how to do this right. We should do all those tests in the constructor and not let a `DataTransfer` object come into existence if any of its prerequisites are not met. We consider the case that everything works out nicely as the normal case and every failure case as exceptional. When a prerequisite fails, we throw an exception inside the constructor because a `DataTransfer` object with unfulfilled prerequisites would not be usable for transferring data anyhow. Listing 6.7 shows how much more readable and therefore also maintainable such a design is in its usage.

Listing 6.7: Usage of better DataTransfer class

```
try {
    DataTransfer dataTransfer = new DataTransfer(connection);
    dataTransfer.transferData(payload);
    dataTransfer.tearDown();
} catch (Exception e) {
    // inform user about what went wrong
}
```

The code for a client of the `DataTransfer` class is now much more understandable because the happy path is very clear with three lines not disrupted with control logic and the unhappy path is dealt with in the catch block. If you do not know what to do with the exceptions that the constructor can throw, you just let the exception propagate up the call stack and let it be handled at a higher level. Of course, production quality code has to deal with all those unhappy paths![4]

Loose coupling

Loose coupling is a well-known design principle. You shield client code from concrete implementations by letting it rely solely on interfaces. In the case of the example about the `DataTransfer` class in the last section you would instead use a `DataTransferInterface` in the client code and this can be used for different network protocols or even transfer by horse if you like.

Other important decoupling principles are asynchronous calls and queuing. You don't get an immediate response in this way, which implies that you need to have some callback mechanism in place which allows the service provider to notify the client about the result of the requested work. Queues also have their place, but you should follow the advice from the section about avoiding complexity.

[4] Exceptions let us program for the happy cases and not clutter the code everywhere with the—necessary!—unhappy cases. For an example from the view of programming paradigms, see Peter Van Roy's piece "Programming Paradigms for Dummies: What Every Programmer Should Know" (Van Roy 2024).

If you need to decouple some sender from the receiver doing the work, a message queue can be a good choice. If you do not need to distribute the work on the receiving side across multiple workers, a streaming design might be the better choice. For example, it is not a good idea to create several workers to write to a database when a single worker already saturates the write capacity of the database.

Consistency

There is this famous example from database transactions. When transferring money from one account to another, the result should be that the amount is deducted from the source account and added to the destination account. Or it should not happen at all, e.g., when the source account does not have enough funds.

It should never happen that the money vanishes from the source account and does not arrive at the destination, or that it appears on the destination account and is not deducted from the source account. That is what is meant by consistency. It immediately follows that you should not create APIs that allow such inconsistent states.

Therefore, you want to stay away from using two calls to achieve such a result, one for withdrawing and one for depositing. In the case that one of the calls is not executed or executed with an error, an inconsistent state results. It is much easier to guarantee consistency by having one call that performs the transaction. It needs all necessary parameters, in this case source account, destination account and amount.

Idempotency

In an ideal world, everything would work out as imagined. We transfer some information to another system, and it should be processed exactly once. But there are all kinds of nastiness that can happen. The calls fail loud and clear without any effect on the target system. Or it is processed partially, and we find out via the result of the call.

Or it is not processed correctly, but gives us no indication that something is wrong. Or it is processed correctly, but we do not get a confirmation. There are lots of reasons why we want to retry our call. In the case that it worked out correctly, calling it again should not change the result. This behavior is called "Idempotency". Retrying a partially successful call should result in the desired end state when the cause for partial failure (e.g., a full disc or a power outage) is gone.

This fulfills not exactly the definition of Idempotency, but you should strive for such a behavior when you design the communication between systems. Consider an e-commerce system where you put articles in a shopping cart and place your order. If the order cannot be completed, you want a retry not to result in getting more of the items in your basket, but you want the order to arrive exactly as it was intended. Using database transactions to implement this behavior helps a lot. Since there is no transaction context between client and server on the Internet context, you can only rely on database transactions in a single request. Otherwise, you need to deal with compensating transactions or at-most-once message protocols. Logging will help to uncover mistakes in your implementation.

6.2.7. Don't Waste Resources

We will discuss an example about responsible use of resources. It wastes resources in four dimensions! We see how this can be improved by a pragmatic implementation, resulting in much less wasteful consumption of resources.

The most common resources our software needs include CPU, memory, disk space, network connections, network bandwidth, database connections and more. It is important to realize that there are no unlimited resources and that they don't come for free. E.g., a database connection needs time to establish, and it needs memory resources on the database server.

Listing 6.8: Ill performing variant selector code

```
function HashMap<String, String> getVariantSelector
        (String articleNumber) {
    List<Article> articleList =
        loadArticleVariants(articleNumber);
    HashMap<String, String> selectors;
    foreach (articleList: Article article) {
        String selector = "Size:␣" + article.size
                        + ",␣Color:␣" + article.color
                        + "Height:␣" + article.height;
        selectors.put(article.articleNumber, selector);
    }
    return selectors;
}
```

The time to establish a connection can vary widely between different database management systems, so with some it is good practice to recycle them between usages by using connection pools. Since databases are shared resources, you should not hog them but hand them back as soon as you don't need them anymore so other requests can get their turn.

To be more concrete, I want to discuss a specific example which wastes resources in four different dimensions at once. Imagine a software which needs to handle variations of a product, e.g., a web shop or a product management system. A product variant is a complex business object which has a significant memory footprint and is also expensive to construct from a database record, that contains information like name, description, universal article number, price, tax, weight, size, color, and much more.

The code in listing 6.8 loads a list with all variants of a certain product. It then creates a selector for selecting a specific variant by extracting the variant information from this list. This looks sensible, and any decent OO programmer would probably agree that this is the way to go.

However, it has a lot of flaws. When you operate it, the database needs to retrieve more information than needed, namely full data sets for variant articles. This takes up more database resources than necessary. It uses

Listing 6.9: Better performing variant selector code

```
function HashMap<String, String> getVariantSelector
    (String articleNumber) {
    PreparedStatement s = DatabaseConnection.prepare(
        "SELECT␣articleNumber,␣size,␣color,␣height
␣FROM␣articles
␣WHERE␣masterNumber␣=␣?"
    );
    ResultSet rs = s.execute([articleNumber]);
    HashMap<String, String> selectors;
    foreach (rs: Row r) {
        String selector = "Size:␣" + r.size
                        + ",␣Color:␣" + r.color
                        + "Height:␣" + r.height;
        selectors.put(r.articleNumber, selector);
    }
    return selectors;
}
```

more network bandwidth than needed, since it transfers more data over the network between the database and application server than necessary.

It uses much more memory and CPU on the application server than needed. An approach using fewer resources is shown in listing 6.9. The first variant might be defended as being more object-oriented. I think this is an ideological argument, considering how few resources the second variant uses. In a real-world case, where a product had 10,000 variants, this resulted in a reduction in processing time from 10 seconds to 1 second, which makes a significant difference.

Furthermore, the list of article objects is only used for this one calculation and not for anything else. It lives only on the stack frame of the function `getVariantSelector` and will be garbage collected when this function returns. Often, such programming constructs are dealt with in operation by increasing resources, like getting a bigger database server and increasing memory per request, but that has other bad consequences besides not really solving the processing time issue.

Listing 6.10: Display location with weather

```
function DisplayData displayLocation(Location location) {
    Weather weather =
        WeatherService.getWeatherForLocation(location);
    LocationData locationData =
        getLocationDataFromDatabase(location);
    DisplayData displayData =
        render(locationData, weather);
    return displayData;
}
```

If you increase memory per request, you can deal with fewer requests at a given time if you do not have more memory in your application server. So it is important to understand the resource consumption of your code. It is not always possible to compensate for bad resource usage by operating more and more hardware. At some point, you can no longer run your application profitably.

Of course, we could push the whole work to the database, and this might be a worthwhile further optimization. It really depends on how we want to distribute the load between database and application server.

6.2.8. Limit Damage

I now want to touch the vast topic of damage control. This is the art of keeping your software up and being useful under adverse conditions, like an external service that behaves bad or can't take the load we put on it. Hopefully, I can whet your appetite to learn more on damage control.

Let's create a fictitious example of a vacation booking application, which displays the weather conditions of the travel destination as an added benefit. Of course, weather data is not the scope of your booking application, so you pull this data from an external weather service. It does not really matter which protocol you use, there will always be some latency for the external service to deliver the weather data for a given location (see listing 6.10).

Well, that is pretty naïve. The `WeatherService` is a remote service and a lot can go wrong when dealing with such beasts. You might not be able to establish a connection, it might take a long time to respond, or the response might be on time, but indicate an error or the response might be invalid altogether.

We have to take care of all of those cases to have a robust application! We might want to display something like "No weather data currently available", when we cannot connect. So we need to deal with a `ConnectionException` in order to achieve this.

But let's focus on a more insidious problem: The service takes longer than usual to respond, perhaps because it is so good that other applications than our own are using it besides. We notice that we are getting more and more `TimeoutExceptions` because the service takes longer than, say, 5 seconds to respond.

We find out that we can change the default timeout to something bigger, let's say 20 seconds. Happy that we found a solution, we rebuild our application with a bigger timeout but sadly, we made things even worse! A lot of people like using our service, but it can't be used anymore at all. What has happened?

Imagine our application server has been set up to handle 1,000 concurrent requests, and it happily did so when the weather service responded quickly within the 5-second standard timeout. Inside maybe 100 milliseconds most of the time. However, there are now times when it takes longer than 5 seconds, so we tried to increase the timeout.

The trouble is that soon our 1,000 web workers will be all used up when 1,000 people hit our service at once. People will hit reload and our service will refuse to connect because there are no more web workers available. The browser will tell the users that our service is not available, and we do not even have any load issue on our service. CPU and database are basically idle, but all our web workers are just waiting for the `WeatherService` to deliver weather data.

You might guess it: Increasing the number of web workers is not really the way out of this situation. Increasing the timeout also wasn't a good idea in the first place. A better idea is to define an acceptable short limit and not increase the timeout beyond that. You might want to also just display "No weather data currently available" in this case.

Nevertheless, if too many requests exceed this acceptable limit, your application might degrade in an unacceptable way. All requests are slow and people will move away from your service. In the end, weather data might be nice to have, but being able to book in a timely manner might be more important. This is why we want to go even further and build in some damage control.

We might want to completely forgo calling the weather service by having a circuit breaker. In the simplest case, this can be something that can be activated by an operator. A more advanced version will trigger automatically as soon as there are more than a few occasional hiccups in the weather service.

You can also build in an automatic reactivation by continuously monitoring the weather service and turning on your emergency switch when the response times are back at an acceptable level. Of course, everything does not need to be black or white. You can still provide the service to some user group for which the ratio of latency vs. usefulness of having the data displayed is good.

The above is only the very beginning of damage control. If you would like to learn more, I highly recommend reading "Release It!".[5] Michael T. Nygard really is the master of damage control. You find more stability patterns like Bulkheads, Steady State, Fail Fast, Let It Crash, Handshaking

[5]Nygard 2018

and others. Also, a lot of experience in developing, operating and stabilizing highly scalable systems. Or you might outsource fault-tolerance by using a service mesh proxy like Istio.

6.2.9. Increase Analyzability

Analyzability is a crucial part of preparedness. When something starts to go wrong, being able to analyze your code quickly will save your neck. I discuss how you can actually have some objective criteria for the analyzability of your software by measuring the cyclomatic complexity. I also mention the importance of your version control history to understand how some problem came into your code base and where you get the most benefit from refactoring.

I often hear developers say that they prefer to rewrite a piece of software instead of trying to understand and fix it or extend it properly. Sometimes the code is really hard to understand, and sometimes people shy away from it because they think it is old and not following the latest conventions and not using the most recent libraries and constructs of the programming language.

However, such an attitude is dangerous. Joel Spolsky describes this very well in his article "Things You Should Never Do, Part I".[6] He tells the story of the rewrite of the Netscape browser which almost killed the complete market share. The reason can be summarized as "too little, too late". Rewriting a code base because you have a hard time understanding it is always a very risky proposition.

Often some ugly piece of code you do not immediately understand solves some important run-time issue or some edge case and has a very good reason to be in this code base. When you rewrite this, you will lose all the investment that has gone into the legacy code base.

[6] Spolsky 2000

In the meantime, your competitors will not sleep and eat into your market share. So when (and if!) you finally come out with your shiny new software, you will almost certainly lack features, performance and robustness. It is unlikely that anybody, who doesn't need to, will use it. Joel has collected his writings in the book "Joel on Software"[7] which contains a lot of valuable experiences and insights.

But how to get out of this predicament? Well, first of all, don't be afraid of code you did not write yourself. If it is used in production, it obviously is of value. Therefore, it is worth keeping and improving its value. Software metrics can be helpful to improve the code.

There is a famous quote attributed to Linus Torvalds. In the early days of Linux, there was a heated debate about how many spaces should be used to indent code. Linus insisted on eight spaces, despite some opposing voices who feared that they could not write deeply nested code in this way. Linus won the argument by saying that deeply nested code is wrong anyway.

I remember being deeply impressed by this anecdote, since I was awestruck by deeply nested code in my early days as a programmer. I also wrote such code back then. When you think about complexity, this rule starts making sense. An often used measure is cyclomatic complexity, which I want to explain looking at a simple piece of code shown in listing 6.11.

[7] Spolsky 2004

Listing 6.11: Simple branching code example

```
if (c1()) {
    f1();
} else {
    f2();
}

if (c2()) {
    f3();
} else {
    f4();
}
```

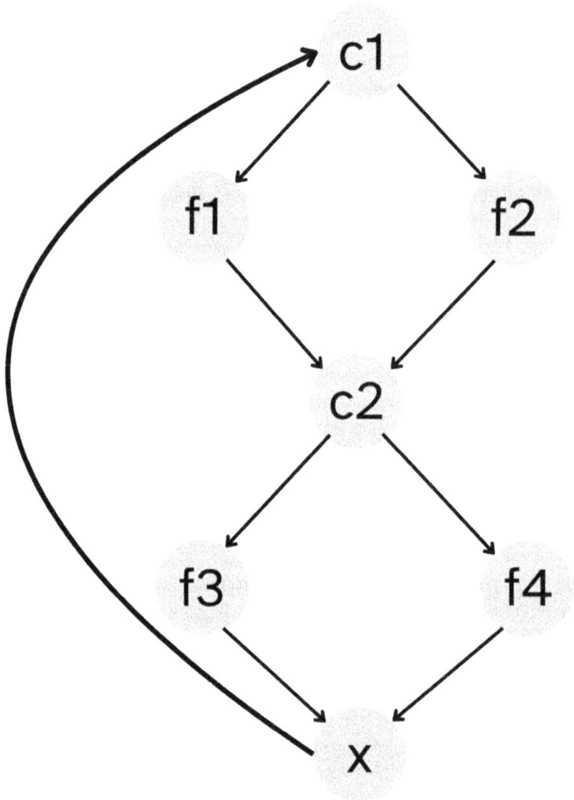

Figure 6.4.: Simple Control-Flow

Graphically, this can be represented with the control-flow graph shown in figure 6.4 (The exit point X is connected to the entry point to make the graph strongly connected). The cyclomatic complexity is defined as[8]

$M = E - N + 2P$[9],

where

E = the number of edges of the graph.
N = the number of nodes of the graph.
P = the number of connected components.

So this can be easily measured by some code analysis tool. But what to do with this number? According to McCabe, who developed this concept, we can distinguish the following cases:

- 1 - 10 Simple procedure, little risk
- 11 - 20 More complex, moderate risk
- 21 - 50 Complex, high risk
- > 50 Untestable code, very high risk

So you can use code analysis tools to check whether your code follows some uniform style and whether you keep its complexity under control. Following clear design principles like SOLID[10] and using names that clearly signify what the purpose of a variable, method, or class is, helps your fellow developer and yourself when you need to fix or extend your code.

[8] *Cyclomatic complexity* 2023

[9] A connected component is a set of nodes connected by edges with no connection to another connected component. In this way, a graph can be decomposed into its connected components.

[10] SOLID stands for the five design principles Single Responsibility Principle, Open/-Closed Principle, Liskov Substitution Principle, Interface Segregation Principle and Dependency Inversion Principle.

As you saw in our example in the section about avoiding flexibility, it is a good idea to avoid setter methods and design immutable objects as much as you can. For understanding a larger code base, it is really helpful to know that an instance of an immutable class cannot change its state outside the place in the code where it was born. That makes reasoning about the code base a lot easier.

Nowadays, we use version control systems to manage our software development and likely also some requirement management system. Some day we might see those two systems converge, but they are mostly separate systems.

You can often integrate the more established systems and if you follow the good practice of starting each of your commits with the requirement id from your requirement system this integration can immediately connect your commits with their corresponding requirement and vice versa. Even if you do not have or use such an integration, you still can use this method to connect commits back to the requirements they stem from by yourself.

This capability is invaluable when you try to find out why a certain change in the software happened at all. If this change causes trouble (e.g., use cases behave just wrong or the performance or resource consumption is not good) you can find out what the reason for the change originally was, which will help you to concoct a fix for this change, which will improve it towards what was intended originally.

While talking about version control, I also want to mention the very interesting book "Software Design X-Rays" by Adam Tornhill.[11] Roughly speaking he makes use of the treasure trove of the history of version control systems to find the hot spots of your software (in the sense of where the most people do the most changes). And where it pays off the most to focus your refactoring efforts. This is highly recommended because it will

[11] Tornhill 2018

transform your code base into a much more manageable form and thereby help a lot in maintaining it.

6.2.10. Increase Visibility

Often, I have the impression that some developers try to hide the inner workings of their creation and to cover their tracks. That's a very bad idea when it comes to understanding why something isn't behaving as expected. You will need your software to be prepared to give a detailed account of what it is doing. So you can efficiently reason about the mismatch between expectation and reality.

We have already discussed the usefulness of logging and observability tools to gain insights into the operation of our software. Let's discuss this a bit further. Logging goes a long way if you have a single server where all the action is.

If your system needs to integrate with other systems by doing synchronous or asynchronous processing, it is a good idea to always log information about the status of batch processes (see subsection 4.2.7) and to log all errors that happen. There is nothing more annoying than silently swallowing exceptions. Errors will go unnoticed and leave you scratching your head.

For synchronous processing (remote calls to external services) you also want to log the full request/response payload on log level debug. This will help you analyze problems when no obvious error is detected but still something goes wrong.

Very often, it is just some wrong assumption about what actually was contained in a request payload. Having the full payload also allows you to copy the request and replay it in your development environment for a more detailed analysis of what really happens in the code.

Logging still is useful when the number of your application nodes grows beyond one. At some point, you might want to collect your logging data in a centralized space to make it easier to analyze.

Log your stuff at the right logging level. A debug info should be logged at log level debug and not on log level error just because you don't remember how to crank up your log level to debug! The default log level of a web application should, of course, be info.

Contrary to that, I saw such a product which was delivered with default log level error. The reason for this probably was, that it spit out a lot of warning messages on any higher level. Of course, you should strive to make your application warning free. There should be no warning because of bad programming style or undefined variables. When you operate at log level error, you miss all logging information on info level, which could be crucial for analyzing incidents.

Logging isn't just for the moment. It will help you analyze problems that lie in the past. You will severely hamper this ability if you mix up your log levels! You should educate your team how to do correct and useful logging.

Monitoring is helpful, too. It should not only be used to check hardware and operating system level data. You should not shy away from putting application level SLIs (service level indicators) into your monitoring setup. You will see if an upgrade of your software improves or worsens the response times for certain parts that you measure with your monitoring system. If you have defined SLOs (service level objectives) you will get an immediate warning if your response times increase above a defined level.

When you have to go into the direction of a heavily distributed architecture (e.g. microservices) you need some way to observe the flow of your request through a complex system.

There are things like the Istio[12] service mesh, which allows you to retrofit your services with a proxy that not only gives you this insight, but much more like traffic management and security. When you have no control over the innards of your services, something like this might be your only hope. Of course, it adds to the complexity of the platform. But it's probably worth it when the alternative would be to be blind.

If you have control over your individual services, you can instrument them to work with distributed tracing tools like Jaeger[13] or even go the route described in "Observability Engineering".[14]

For comprehensive insight into how your software operates, you can use a patched version of Linux and gain profound insights into the system calls of your software with KUTrace. With so little overhead that you can even use this on a production system.[15]

6.2.11. Increase Robustness

I want to explain why you want to invest into the robustness of your software. I illustrate the topic with a real-life incident, which provides several learnings. What you should do on a technical and organizational level to resolve incidents and, most importantly, what measures to take to prevent them from re-occurring.

First, I want to describe a typical setup in today's IT operations. Often, companies outsource a lot of IT skills and focus on their core business, like manufacturing or trading. They still need to develop custom software for their business, and they also need to operate it. But they would rather not hire and employ those highly specialized people.

[12] *Istio Service Mesh* 2023
[13] *Jaeger: open source, distributed tracing platform* 2023
[14] Majors, Fong-Jones, and Miranda 2022
[15] Sites 2022

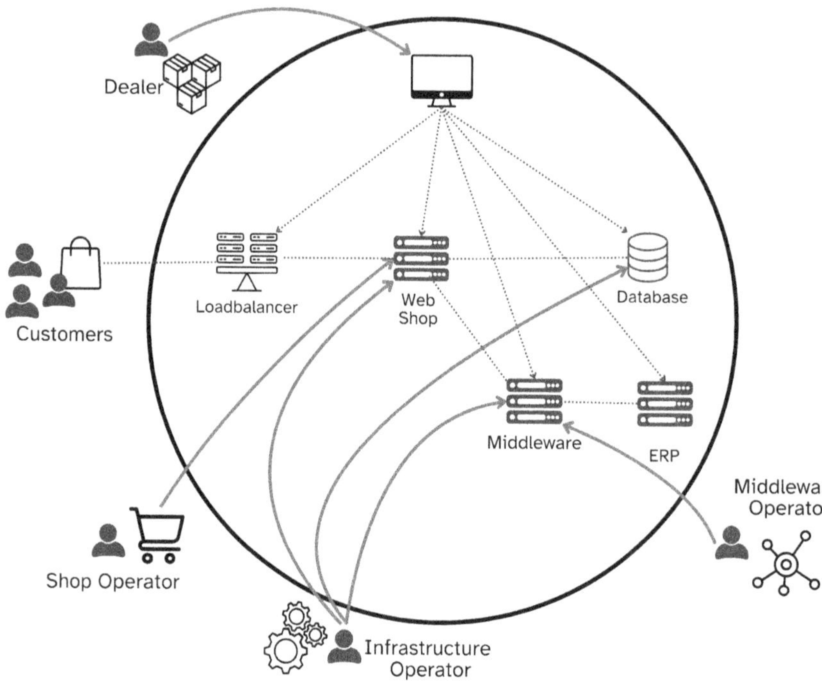

Figure 6.5.: Operation Responsibility Graph

Often, they need development skills only for the limited duration of a project and operational skills only for a few hours per month, so it makes no sense for them to permanently hire those people. I work for a company offering customization and application support for a web shop software. We often cooperate with infrastructure specialists employed with still another company to help with the setup and operation of the infrastructure.

Also, we work with a middleware company, helping to customize and operate their middleware for integration with the ERP system. In the case I want to describe here, the whole IT of this business is operated in a cloud and the only one with access to the cloud management system is the business itself, which I will call "dealer" to avoid misunderstandings.

The cloud management cockpit offers things like resources available to the individual servers, connection management (which servers in the dealer's IT can talk to each other), configuration of the load balancer (which is the entry point into the web shop for customers from the Internet) and shutdown and reboot of individual servers. The operation responsibility graph shown in figure 6.5 illustrates this situation.

This diagram tries to visualize that the shop system could be viewed as consisting of the shop server with an underlying database management system and an attached middleware to connect it to an ERP system. The infrastructure people manage the infrastructure issues like installing the operating system and services like web server and database management system and keeping everything secure by installing security patches.

We from the shop company take care of application level issues with our software, the middleware people take care of their middleware. To enable this, everyone has SSH access to those systems he is responsible for. Just the other day I got a message from the dealer. His customers couldn't use his web shop anymore. Instead of seeing the shop, the customers were only confronted with an error page saying that a web server got no response while acting as a gateway.

I could immediately confirm this, but it was even worse, I could not connect via HTTPS to the web shop system and also not via SSH. The only thing I could tell the dealer at this stage was that only his IT or the cloud provider could help, since I did not have access to the cloud management front-end. Our infrastructure guys confirmed this was the way to proceed, but also wondered why the web shop was down for already an hour without their monitoring giving an alert.

This provided the first lesson of the incident: I told infrastructure that we need to hear about such incidents first from their monitoring and not from the dealer who gets complaints from his customers. We want to be able to notify the dealer that we are working on a solution before they even get complaints from their customers! The middleware people told us that they also got no sign of life from the web shop, but their middleware which connected the web shop to the ERP system was up and running.

Finally, the dealer (who has access to the cloud management front-end) was able to restart the web shop system and signaled that all was clear again. Sadly, that wasn't the case. An hour later, the next devastating message came from the dealer. The orders placed in the web shop did not arrive in the ERP system.

I checked and could only say that the middleware indeed hadn't pulled a single order for the last few hours. This problem, however, had to wait for the next day to be resolved, since nobody from middleware was available anymore. Of course, the problem got resolved first thing in the morning and the project manager announced that luckily the crisis was over.

And this is the second lesson from this incident: A manual restart of a single component won't resolve problems that involve several different software components with different stakeholders. There is often no mechanism to notify dependent components that such a restart has happened and that it should react appropriately, perhaps also with a re-initialization.

However, you should never let a good crisis go to waste. Therefore, I told the project manager, that the crisis is not over until all the learnings have happened and that two unhappy paths that failed were improved in such a way, that they would not fail again. This means that the monitoring gives an alert when the system is down (should be a given, shouldn't it?) and also that the middleware automatically resumes processing when the system comes back to life.

Ensuring that such unhappy paths work is essential for distributed systems. How to implement happy paths is described in any textbook, but unhappy paths behaving sensibly are what really makes your day in real life. An incident is not over when stuff accidentally works again.

This is the starting point for making sure that the same incident creates less damage when it will happen again (and it is really a question of "when" and not "if"). In the case of the middleware not pulling orders from the web shop anymore despite being up and running: it turned out that it was still waiting for an HTTP request to deliver a response, which never came because the server crashed before it could finish processing. Infinite timeouts are never a good idea.

The third and most important lesson is that you need to actively take care if you want to build a highly available distributed system involving different stakeholders. You need to extend your DevOps mindset beyond the confines of your own organization. You must constantly strive for every involved party to feel responsible for the whole and not only for their own part. There just is no place for a "not my business" mentality in our times.

6.2.12. Respect your Legacy

I conclude the second part with a few words about respecting your legacy. Legacy code is often regarded as being old and rotten and not being worth your time. You should be respectful. Often, it is this legacy code which earns the money your company needs to pay your wages. Therefore, it should be considered valuable and treated with respect. Chances are that it will outlast your stay at the company.

Many developers prefer working on the implementation of so-called greenfield projects, which start with no code legacy whatsoever. Sometimes you have no other option because there is no operational application yet. But in many cases, there is. I have mentioned the story of the Netscape rewrite as told by Joel Spolsky.[16]

Most of the time, you have neither the budget nor the time to do a greenfield restart. This is true despite existing counter examples. A famous counter example is the development of the Apple Macintosh, while Apple

[16] Spolsky 2000

was still doing successful business with the Apple II. But it is dangerous to think that you can also be successful with a restart.

For every success, there are countless failures. Even at Apple, it was not only the Macintosh project which turned out successful. Around the same time, they developed the Lisa, which failed. I have often heard people at conferences telling about some greenfield project which would clean up the whole mess at an enterprise and make life better for everyone.

Most of the time, the same people did not appear in the following years at the same conference to report about their success. In my view, hearing how something has been implemented is much more interesting than some cloudy ideas about how it is intended to be done.

Why is it so that developers don't like legacy code? Surely, it is much easier to write code than to read it. For this reason, I advocate to take every effort to counter this effect and write code with readability and maintainability in mind.

But there is an even more important aspect: The productive code earns its keep, and it generates the revenue needed to pay for maintenance or fresh development. Often, software development isn't the core business and therefore the resources in terms of available people and money are limited.

If you redirect too much of your resources towards some greenfield project, you lack the same resources for maintaining your business. This might put you in a situation where you are not able to compete in the market anymore. That's why I think we should really not look down on legacy software, even if it is not in a perfect shape. We should always be respectful because it earns the money that pays our wages.

In most cases, we should improve it on every step of the way and permanently overhaul it. This way, we keep the investment that has been made into the legacy software and make it more valuable over time. A good read

Figure 6.6.: The Hare and the Hedgehog by Otto Ubbelohde (1909)

about how to work with legacy code is “Working Effectively with Legacy Code”.[17]

I like to compare the development of a greenfield project with the intention to supersede a legacy project to the story of the hare and the hedgehog (figure 6.6). The hedgehog bets against a hare that he can outrun him, and the hare takes the bet, since he just knows that he is the faster animal.

The hedgehog only runs a few steps, but at the goal his wife who looks very similar to the hedgehog waits for the hare and calls “I'm already here”. The hare wants revenge and tries in vain to outrun the hedgehog for 73 times and collapses on the 74th attempt and dies.

It is very similar with greenfield projects trying to outpace a legacy project. If they aren't killed before they reach their first release, this first release is like a baby. It is lacking in features, performance, and stability and all in all, is much less capable than the legacy project.

Just as a baby, it needs to learn to walk and talk. But while maturing, the legacy project is still in use and maintained. It gains new features, bugs

[17]Feathers 2009

are fixed, performance is improved. So when the greenfield project reaches its next release, it is still a worse choice than the legacy project. The odds are that it will be exhausted sooner than in 74 iterations and die.

Part III.

Evolution on the Organizational Level

7. Overview

In the software industry, it is now widespread knowledge, that although there is no silver bullet, it is possible to achieve much better results. We can deliver software faster, more reliable and with fewer errors than it was thought possible in the not so distant past. The tool to achieve such a high-performance organization is DevOps. But you won't do DevOps justice by viewing it as a set of technical capabilities which you can employ as a new function in your enterprise. DevOps is much more about a cultural transformation.

I will review (very briefly) research results which clearly show the connection of DevOps practices and cultural transformation to achieving a high-performance organization. You can read more about this research in the book 'Accelerate' by Nicole Forsgren, Jim Humble and Gene Kim.[1]

In this book, and elsewhere, you will also find that it is thought that "DevOps works best for in-house projects". Probably due to the intended cultural changes.

I do have some experience with in-house software projects, but when I first came across DevOps, I was exclusively working in contract projects. From my experience, I would add to this statement a "but it can also work in contract situations". It just is not a given, and I think the key to succeeding in contract situations lies in integrating the customer (or contracting entity) in every one of the three pillars of DevOps (this goes way beyond customer participation in Agile).

[1] Forsgren, Humble, and Kim 2018

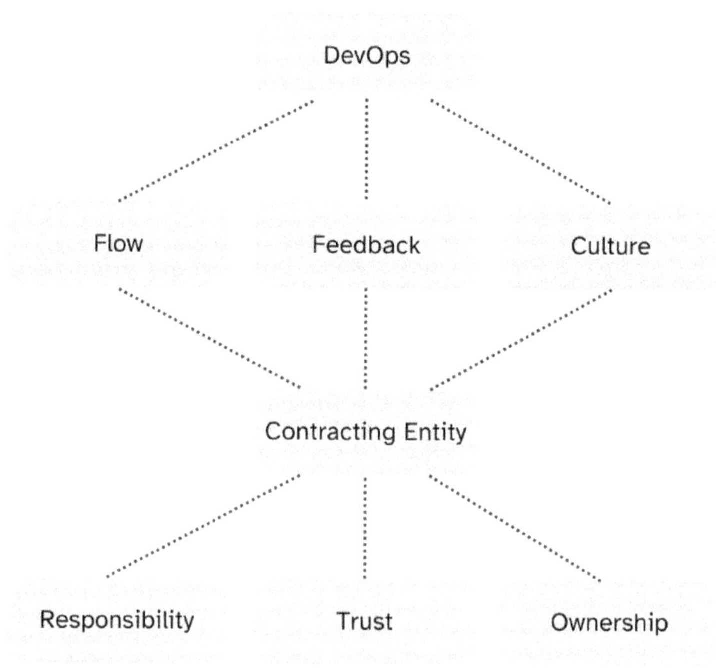

Figure 7.1.: DevOps Beyond In-house

The customer must be an integral part of your software delivery flow, it is of utmost importance to have a well-established feedback loop with the customer, and it is imperative to align cultural values and to establish a common learning meta-organization. To embed the anecdotal stories, I want to tell in this cultural setting, I also give a brief introduction to the cultural typology by Ron Westrum and describe a few cultural values I believe are especially important for succeeding with DevOps beyond in-house projects.

8. High Performance Organizations

Scientific research shows (again, see the very enlightening book "Accelerate"[1] by Forsgren, Kim and Humble), that the implementation of DevOps practices is positively correlated with high performance organizations. The research is based on survey data that was grouped into clusters by so-called cluster analysis. The variables examined were deployment frequency, lead time for changes, mean time to recovery (MTTR) and change failure rate.

The clusters that emerged showed that the organizations in the high performance cluster did significantly better than the medium and low performers in all observed variables, and that the medium performers did significantly better than the low performers in all observed variables. Interestingly, tables 8.1 and 8.2 show, that high software delivery performance is not related to a higher error rate, but that the opposite is true. Often, there still exists "deployment fear" which is expressed as "don't deploy on Fridays" or "only deploy on fixed days".

When I hear such concerns, I usually reply that it is completely the other way round and that the deployment has to be so robust that you can trigger it on Saturday night and be confident that nothing breaks. The deployment has to deliver the full system and the correct configuration of the target. It also needs to make sure that services respond correctly to the changes.

This might be done by reloading or restarting a service (a "good" service like the Apache web server understands the signal SIGHUP[2] and reacts

[1] Forsgren, Humble, and Kim 2018

[2] SIGHUP is the hangup signal, which is interpreted by background processes in UNIX-like operating systems to signify that the process should reload its configuration.

by reloading its configuration. Sometimes deployment processes are not complete and, e.g., only deliver the source code but not the configuration. After deployment, you need to manually configure the system. This is of course not what I mean when I use the term "deployment process"! A deployment process is only usable once it is a 'push one button' solution.

DevOps research clearly shows that the fear of breaking something and therefore being reluctant with software delivery is unfounded. You do not get higher error rates when you are capable of delivering on demand. If deployment is painful for you, you should not evade the pain, but you should do it more often to develop your "delivery muscles". Once those muscles are strong enough, it won't hurt anymore to use them.

Another research result is that DevOps works best for in-house development and not so much for outsourced contract projects. This does by no means imply that in-house development is a guarantee for success. I remember several occasions, where I was asked to consult some dealers who used a customized web shop software and experienced issues with some third-party modules.

What I found, was sobering: There was no development environment, where you could debug the issues. There was no automatic deployment, not to speak of a usable test system or a delivery pipeline. The in-house developers were just directly modifying the productive system! When asked about a test system, they admitted having one, but that it wasn't in a shape to be used.

Of course, they never knew if activating or deactivating a third-party module would bring down their productive system. They had no way of finding out if such a module was compatible with their customized system other than doing open-heart surgery. There were booby traps everywhere and job frustration was very high. It was no surprise that nobody stayed for longer than he needed to find another job.

Nevertheless, I do not believe that an in-house setting is a necessary prerequisite for successful projects. On the contrary, I think you just need a few more organizational ingredients to be successful with DevOps in contract projects.

Table 8.1.: Software Delivery Performance for 2016

2016	**High Performers**	**Medium Performers**	**Low Performers**
Deployment Frequency	On demand (multiple deploys per day)	Between once per week and once per month	Between once per month and once every six months
Lead Time for Changes	Less than one hour	Between one week and one month	Between one month and six months
MTTR	Less than one hour	Less than one day	Less than one day
Change Failure Rate	0–15%	1–45%	6–30%

Table 8.2.: Software Delivery Performance for 2017

2017	**High Performers**	**Medium Performers**	**Low Performers**
Deployment Frequency	On demand (multiple deploys per day)	Between once per week and once per month	Between once per week and once per month
Lead Time for Changes	Less than one hour	Between one week and one month	Between one week and one month
MTTR	Less than one hour	Less than one day	Between one day and one week
Change Failure Rate	0–15%	0–15%	31–45%

An important research finding is, that high performance of an organization correlates with its culture. Very shortly, there exists a classification of organizations into three types. The first type is dominated by power, the second by rules, and the third are learning organizations. The research finding is that high-performance organizations belong to the third category, and that the other two categories are not able to achieve on-demand delivery, but instead delay or block the timely delivery of changes. I will provide a more detailed description of the three types of organizational cultures, according to Ron Westrum.

The interesting question is why DevOps is mostly successful with in-house projects and less often with contractual situations involving several organizations. Even more interesting, I believe you can be successful with DevOps in projects involving several organizations.

Then I will list a few principles which, I think, are important for successfully implementing DevOps in any project, but even more so in contractual situations where you want to achieve high performance. And I will also describe a few projects where I think that the lack of implementation of those principles have hindered the projects or how the presence of those has enabled the success of certain projects.

The examples follow roughly the three types of organizational culture. In the last example, the project could be considered as a highly performing one.

I try to reflect on how the different stakeholders can work together and how the different cultures influence the project and how the project even influences the culture of the organizations.

9. Organizational Culture

The research presented in "Accelerate"[1] clearly shows a correlation of organizational culture with the capability of high-performance software delivery. The DevOps movement also clearly understands that it is in a large part about culture.

The first pillar of DevOps, Flow, has a big technical dimension. The second pillar, Feedback, has technical aspects, but also a significant cultural dimension. Even more important than the feedback gained from technical systems is the feedback from the customer to verify that our work is of value to him. And, last but not least, the third pillar, Continuous Improvement, is about a culture of constant learning.

Ron Westrum created a framework for classifying the values and principles of organizations. This framework helps in understanding how the most successful organizations function. Westrum classifies organizations into three types:[2]

- Pathological Culture: In a pathological culture, there is a lack of trust and openness among employees. Information is hoarded, and power is centralized in the hands of a few individuals. This type of culture inhibits collaboration and innovation, leading to poor performance and low employee satisfaction.
- Bureaucratic Culture: A bureaucratic culture is characterized by strict adherence to rules and procedures. Decision-making is hierarchical, with little autonomy given to employees. While this type of

[1] Forsgren, Humble, and Kim 2018

[2] The definition of the Westrum cultural type is taken from Agile-Ideation 2023.

culture promotes orderliness and stability, it can also stifle creativity and agility.

- Generative Culture: A generative culture fosters an environment of trust, openness, and psychological safety. Employees feel empowered to take risks, share ideas freely, and collaborate across teams. This type of culture encourages learning from mistakes and continuous improvement, leading to high-performance and organizational success.

In Part II, I describe a path mainly relevant for the individual development from apprentice to journeyman. I think there is a similar path which organizations can take on their way to improve their capabilities for delivering better software with shorter time to market and with fewer errors.

I believe organizations can evolve from pathological to bureaucratic to generative. In the best case, even from pathological to generative without becoming bureaucratic on their journey. But I also believe that this evolution is much harder than personal development. It takes a whole bunch of people to move in the same direction!

As already mentioned, research suggests, that DevOps works best in an in-house project. In "Accelerate" it was found, that the better the organizational culture, the better the software delivery performance. From my experience, I believe that this is true, and it can be challenging to transform an organization to adopt a high performance generative culture.

I even believe that the Westrum typology applies to contract projects where at least two organizations are involved. Often there are many more contractors involved and this is even harder, but I believe it is possible, and I want to describe a few experiences, where quite a bit has been achieved in this way.

One cannot emphasize enough that a DevOps culture is not achieved by hiring DevOps engineers. If you are lucky, you will find people who can help you with transformation. But it won't work if your organization does not want to evolve. There has to be management buy-in. Visionary leadership is helpful too, and your staff should want to achieve better outcomes.

Large companies like Amazon or Zalando have chosen to split their workforce into small, independent and decoupled teams. Those teams have no dependencies from other teams and also are the business owner in their area of focus. Technically, they choose microservices architectures. The term 'micro' is a bit misleading, since a microservice typically consists of a full stack of operating system and supporting services like data storage to support the service in question.

The goal is to decouple it completely from other services and only communicate via well-defined APIs. You can read more about the Amazonian way to scale a company in "working backwards" by Colin Bryar and Bill Carr.[3] I think the most important aspect of microservices is nothing technical, but that it allows independent and decoupled teams in large organizations. Without such a decoupling, a large organization would not be able to move forward quickly once it reaches a certain size.

This decoupling of single purpose teams is an important hint to how you can achieve high performance when several contractors are involved. You should strive to form a virtual generative team with your customer and other contractors working on the same delivery, and you should decouple as much as possible from other contributors to not get slowed down by them.

Amazon learned that it is important that their single purpose teams are also the business owners of their focus area.[4] Transferring this insight into a contract situation is actually a tough call. Scrum has the special role of a "product owner" and I believe this role should be filled by a member of the customer organization. Some people advocate for a proxy product owner on the side of the service organization, which is a tempting idea because it superficially allows you to move faster.

[3] Bryar and Carr 2021
[4] Bryar and Carr 2021

But often, this speed turns out to be illusionary when it comes to measuring the real value for the customer. In my experience, the best way is to keep product ownership where it really belongs (namely on the customer side). And strive to integrate the business team and the service team into one team as much as possible. Being able to give direct feedback to the people implementing a requirement and having complete transparency enables the business people to do a fully informed decision of which changes they want to put into production and at what time.

Of course, there are limits to such an integration across organizational boundaries. Business ownership can only be on the customer side. Therefore, the productive system is 'owned' by the business. The delivery pipeline is best owned by the service provider. In this setup, it would be very easy to just roll out changes to the system owned by the customer. You shouldn't do that. We will see from real-life examples later that this is not helpful with building trust.

You should only perform planned changes to a productive system with the informed consent of the customer. Emergency situations are different, since they often require immediate action to prevent downtime and loss.

10. Values for Succeeding in Contract Projects

In this chapter, I list a few values and principles that I believe to be relevant for succeeding with DevOps in a contract project. Of course, those are also helpful for in-house development, but I want to show how you can be successful beyond that. This approach is by no means scientific. It is based on anecdotal material from my personal experience and reflects my personal views.

The values I want to describe in this chapter are:

- Capability to Deliver
- Quality
- Focus on Value for the Customer
- Vision
- Transparency
- Honesty
- Modesty
- Trust
- Feedback
- Ownership
- Communication
- Diligence
- Clear responsibility

10.1. Capability to Deliver

At the heart of DevOps practices is the delivery pipeline. It is formulated in the Flow pillar of DevOps. The delivery pipeline allows you to fully automate the roll-out of changes in your software and configuration. Database schema changes are also considered as configuration changes and are applied automatically to the target system.

If you have to do some manual step to complete a delivery, then your delivery pipeline is not ready for use in a DevOps setting. Software delivery has to become a painless process that can be executed with confidence. If it hurts, do it more often and fix what is causing you pain. It all began with the presentation "10+ deploys per day" by Allspaw and Hammond.[1] I mentioned this presentation before, which already included many of the core concepts of DevOps. This should give a rough orientation of where you want to go. Advanced organizations handle many more deployments per day.

It is a clear sign of "deployment fear". when you hear statements like "we don't deploy on Fridays" or "we only deploy on a certain day of the week" (or even month). There is a fear that the deployment will break the productive system and that you can't fix it quickly enough. The situation will not improve if you do not hone your pipeline to be as reliable as possible. It can make a difference, whether you have to deliver software for your own company or for an external client. In the first case, you might get fired when you work for a pathological company. In the second case, you might need to pay damages. In both cases, you will benefit when your delivery pipeline is reliable.

This capability to delivery becomes even more important when you are not a part of the organization that needs your software. Why should you get paid when you can't deliver value? You need to respect the dividing

[1] Allspaw and Hammond 2009

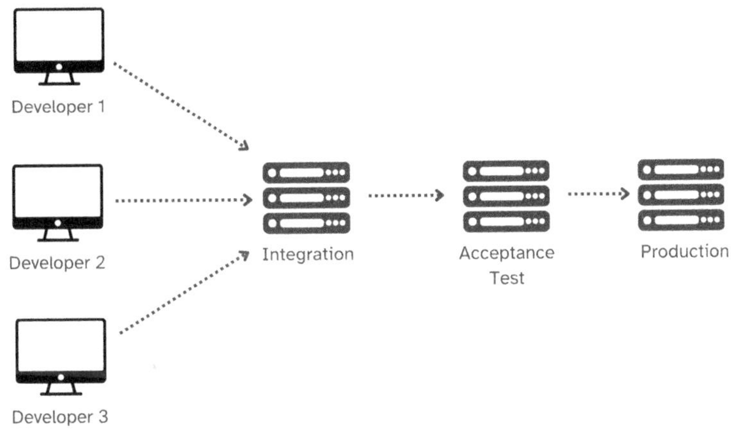

Figure 10.1.: Delivery Process

line between your and the customer's organization, and you need to be aware that you do not own the productive system of your customer. It is really important to get a sign-off from your customer when you deliver your changes. It is also important that you decouple your efforts as much as possible from external dependencies. Needing to wait for someone else to complete their work will slow you down.

10.2. Quality

Quality assurance is really an integral part of the software delivery process. But it is so important that you can't stress it enough, and therefore I devote a separate section to this topic.

Often, there is a naïve view that you just develop a perfect piece of software and then just put it on the productive system and everybody is happy. Unfortunately, what we do is rarely perfect but riddled with all sorts of defects. Some of those can be caught by automatic processes like strictly typed programming languages, code scanners or automatic tests. Of course, we use all those battle-proven mechanisms to make our lives easier.

So why have a delivery process which has to pass several stages of quality assurance or quality gates? A common delivery process is shown in figure 10.1. Several developers contribute features which are integrated on an integration system and acceptance tested on an acceptance test system. The corresponding three quality gates are shown as diamonds in the more detailed figure 10.2. The first one is the code review step, which eliminates issues that are obvious to an experienced developer (Google calls that 'readability' in their book 'Software Engineering at Google').[2]

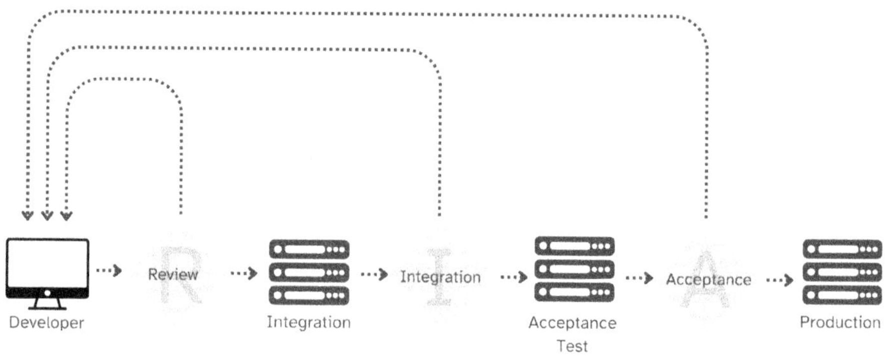

Figure 10.2.: Delivery Process Feedback

When the reviewer finds an error in the code review, it must be fixed (normally by the original developer) and the change is reconsidered. It is only accepted once the reviewer is satisfied. My advice is to carry out reviews suspiciously. Never trust a change just because it was submitted by a more experienced developer. It is not disrespectful to the developer to distrust the code he has written. On the contrary, this is good teamwork. If you don't understand the submitted code, there is no shame in having the developer explain the change to you. Typically, both the reviewer and the

[2]Winters, Manshreck, and Wright 2020

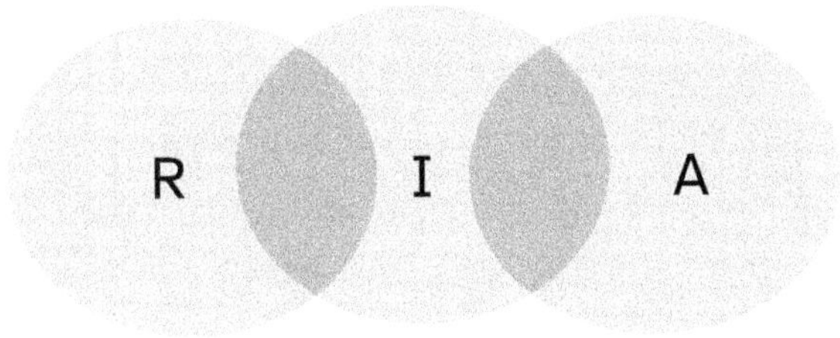

Figure 10.3.: Cumulative Quality Assurance

developer will learn something. The set of errors eliminated at this stage is denoted 'R' in figure 10.3. Once this quality gate is passed, the code change is deployed on the integration system. It is checked whether it works outside the developer machine and if it does not interfere in an unwanted way with the rest of the software system. Only when this quality gate is passed, we can promote the change(s) to the acceptance test system.[3]

If our change does not pass the integration test stage, it needs to *go back to square one* and pass the review quality gate again. The set of errors eliminated in the integration stage is denoted 'I' in figure 10.3. After we hand over our changes on the acceptance test system to the business experts to perform their acceptance tests, we try to pass the acceptance quality gate.[4]

[3]We can therefore view the integration system as an eliminator of the 'works on my machine' effect. Common causes of this effect include forgetting to commit a file belonging to the change or not submitting the correct configuration for the downstream systems.

[4]We can view the acceptance test system as an eliminator of the 'works in my head' effect. This occurs when we have assured that there is no 'works on my machine' effect any more, but the people needing our software have a different understanding of what it should do.

Any error found in the acceptance stage also *puts the offending change back on square one.* After a fix has been made (usually by the original developer), the change has to pass the review quality gate and the integration quality gate once again (both of them!), before it is resubmitted for acceptance testing. Only after it has passed review and integration and acceptance (all three!), we can promote the changes to the production system. The set of errors eliminated in the acceptance test stage is denoted 'A' in figure 10.3.

This strict forward process (this means that there is never a newer version of the software on a downstream system in the delivery pipeline) guarantees that we eliminate as many errors as we can in our software before we put it on the productive system, namely the union of the sets 'R', 'I' and 'A'. In this way, we do our best to ensure the integrity and availability of the productive system. With "strict forward" process, I mean, that a later stage in the delivery process never has a newer version of the software (see figure 10.1). This allows you to confidently reason about the state of your delivery pipeline. You can always be assured that a bug that has been eliminated on the production system will not be present anymore in the previous stages.

When you look at figure 10.2 once more, you see that there are no shortcuts. You can't fix an integration issue just on the integration system or an acceptance test issue on the acceptance test system (or go back only to the integration system, omitting the review step). This would violate the 'strict forward' principle, it would not give you the maximum elimination of errors, and it would rob you of the ability to reason about issues since you no longer have the guarantee that you have the most recent version of the code on your development machine. Don't go there. Here be dragons.[5] And they are hard to kill.

[5] "Here be dragons" signifies dangerous or unexplored territories. You could see those areas marked with dragons on medieval maps.

There are of course exceptions to this rule, namely in the case of emergencies. In emergencies, there can also be exceptions to the "informed consent" rule. In analogy to good medical practice, you will try to save the life of an unconscious patient under the assumption that you are acting in his best interest. Of course, you need to apply any hotfixes you do in this way to the main line at a later point, and they have to propagate through all quality gates this time. This can be done by implementing a trunk-based strategy.[6]

Occasionally, you might wonder if it is worth having a dedicated integration system or even more quality assurance systems. I hope I could convince you that it is a bad idea to go without one if you really care about making your customer happy. Availability and integrity of the productive system are prerequisites to this.

10.3. Focus on Value for the Customer

The ultimate goal is to deliver value for the customer. In a contract setting, this is the company for which you are building software. Try to understand the business needs as well as you can, and don't build stuff that might be useful sometimes. You will need to maintain it, and it will slow you down to deliver when it counts. Instead, build stuff that is actually needed.

Does this mean falling back to the most simple and primitive software? To avoid re-use and flexibility at any price? Of course not, but those are not ends in themselves! If you need flexibility from the beginning, you will build it in from the beginning. If you need it later, you will create it by refactoring. We saw that flexibility has a price that often isn't worth it in subsection 6.2.5. Build what will create actual and not potential value!

[6] In trunk-based development all changes are committed directly to the main branch (also called trunk) and therefore get delivered with every deployment. This requires good test coverage and feature toggles to hide features that take longer to develop than the interval between two deployments.

In subsection 6.2.4, we saw an example, of how the choice of a new software component that the team didn't know how to operate securely and reliably and also had no idea how to correctly integrate it into the customer system created a disproportionate amount of havoc. To refrain from such decisions does not mean that you should not familiarize yourself with new technologies. It just means that you should follow the good medical practice to "first of all, do no harm". Besides reducing cost and saving time, this also helps to deliver quickly. This enables getting feedback early and thereby ensuring that you deliver an actual value for your customer which he can use in turn to improve his business. YAGNI (You Ain't Gonna Need It) applies when you notice you are implementing something that has no value for your customer.

Being clear on this goal also helps you when dealing with people who want to do things in 'the right way' (and not the right things!), as they have always done it. This 'right way' often involves long planning and implementation phases. Often, when you deliver something at all, it will be too little, too late. It is often a matter of assigning your resources to also deal with formal processes at your customer that do not really align with the dynamics of small incremental deliveries. Sometimes, internal processes still assume big one-time deliveries that are 'done' and then checked for security, for example. A better solution is to integrate security scans into your delivery pipeline.

10.4. Vision

You need to have a clear vision of where you want to go. What you want to achieve, how you can approach your goal by doing iterations that bring you closer. You need to align this vision with the needs of your customer, and you must align the entire team with the vision by making them aware of the goal and what needs to be done to reach it. The incapability to align vision across organizational boundaries may be an important reason why

DevOps is often thought to work mainly for in-house development. In a contract situation, you need to have regular alignment meetings with your customer (and other service providers).

The examples in the next chapter reflect on how this can work more or less effectively. From my experience, I think it is best not to proxy the communication with the customer, but to involve all developers. This will enable a common and in-depth understanding. Playing "silent mail" by only letting project managers or business analysts talk to the customer and then relay the insights to the developers will rather hinder this more in-depth understanding.

10.5. Transparency

Transparency is a key value. In a contract project, you can't go without acceptance tests done by the customer. The customer has to know exactly what needs to be tested. Therefore, he needs to have complete transparency about what he gets. One possibility to create transparency is to make release notes available for every release.

Every change should be clearly traceable to the requirement, which triggered the change. The flow of value has to be made visible so that every stakeholder can clearly see what is delivered and what is at which stage in delivery. Transparency is a necessary prerequisite for trust.

10.6. Honesty

Not everything goes as smoothly as we want. We might become aware that we can't make a deadline. We might become aware that we botched up a delivery or that we released some bug that went unnoticed through all our quality gates. The worst thing we can do is to keep quiet and hope that nobody notices. And let the customer realize that we won't be providing what he needs when the deadline is reached.

Of course, there are different customers who deal differently with honest service providers. There are customers who are stuck in a pathological or bureaucratic culture who might want to use this information to punish the service provider or kill the messenger. Which isn't a good idea anyhow. But in my experience, most customers value honesty and will honor it.

To be more explicit: Tell your customer as soon as you can see that you won't be able to deliver on time! The customer needs to be able to react. They need to be able to adjust their plans and their market communication. Furthermore, they need to be able to deal features for budget or time and maybe be able to re-prioritize the requested features that they can still make a hard deadline but deliver some less important features after the deadline.

You rob your customer of all this flexibility if you are not honest about how you view the progress of the project. There can be many reasons why you can't make a deadline. You cannot anticipate the unforeseeable, but you can prepare for it. Without honesty, there probably will be no trust, or it will be lost as soon as it becomes clear that you withheld information.

10.7. Modesty

Nobody knows everything. Do not try to convey the impression that there is an exception to this rule. We build systems that are very complex, making them often difficult to understand and analyze. We should not be overconfident because of this. Please keep in mind that 'pride comes before a fall'. The next fall is just waiting around the corner, and it is better to prepare for it.

We often talk about "best practices". I try to avoid this term altogether and use the more modest term "good practice". How should you improve your practice when it already is "best"? But "best practices" have become so ingrained into our culture that I already spotted the term "better best practices" in print. Go figure.

10.8. Trust

Trust can't be demanded, trust has to be earned. It takes a lot to earn trust. And it can be lost a lot faster than it can be earned. Trust comes from trustworthy behavior. Being transparent, honest and authentic goes a long way to build trust. A trustful relationship with your customers and your implementation partners is essential for creating a generative culture which spans all involved organizations.

Integrating your customer into the delivery process by providing clearly defined releases on the acceptance test system and only deploying to production when the customer has signed off the changes can contribute a lot to a trustful relationship. When the customer has experienced a lot of such deployments with no or only minor surprises, he will handle the sign-off with growing confidence.

Once we needed to replace a legacy system, which was integrated with more than a handful of other systems. A week before the deadline, we still had plenty of open topics. But we were able to release those changes before the deadline in quick succession of sometimes close to 10 releases per day. This customer stated two months after the go-live that he trusts our delivery process. We should constantly strive to make our delivery process so reliable that it is possible to earn this kind of trust.

10.9. Feedback

In a contract setting, feedback is indispensable. We do not discuss feedback from the build process here, which includes unit tests, integration tests, automated acceptance tests, code scans, and the like. You provide a service to a different organization, and there is no way for feedback to diffuse through your organization. It has to cross organizational borders, and therefore special care has to be taken that feedback can flow back to you. Regular reviews with the customer are valuable.

Connecting your changes to customer requirements is essential. You probably use some requirement management system where you have a description of the customer's requirements and where you can discuss the state of completion of a requirement. Sometimes, executable requirements are in use. Those consist of a formal, human-readable requirement definition which is also interpretable by a computer so you can automatically check whether a requirement is fulfilled. I have no experience with executable requirements and therefore cannot say anything about how feasible this is.

10.10. Ownership

In contract projects, it is essential to understand who owns what. The productive system is, of course, owned by the customer, and you should never change the productive system without the consent of the owner. It is like good medical practice. Your physician isn't allowed to treat you without your informed consent. The same goes for a productive system.

It is, of course, important that the customer is aware about the changes planned for the productive system. You need to have an acceptance test system which is as close to the productive system as possible, so the customer can test everything you have provided and decide whether it is good enough to go into production.

This also means that the customer has to be informed about every change made available for acceptance testing. Even if you think a change is not relevant for the customer, it has to be made visible to the customer, e.g.,

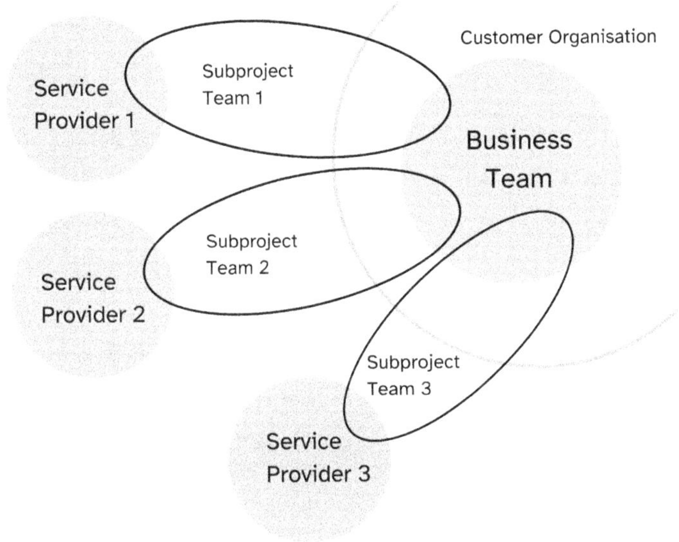

Figure 10.4.: Multiple Service Providers

in the form of release notes. You can only promote your changes to the productive system once they have been signed off by the customer.

When you have contracting companies involved who develop largely independent parts (e.g., a content management system (CMS) and a customer relationship management system (CRM)) it is rather a good idea to have separate delivery pipelines for those independent parts. You will want those parties to move as much independently of each other as possible. But each independent party should be the business owner of its part.

This is obviously not possible for the service provider, since he is not part of the customer's organization. The way out of this predicament is to form an organization-spanning team with the business owners. See figure 10.4 to get an idea of what this can look like for several service providers who form independent project teams with the business owner to supply independent components. Making a conscious effort to not delay deliveries on the service side and to not delay sign-off decisions on the customer side can still result in many successful deployments per day by close cooperation between the involved parties.

Of course, there can be slow-downs in the sign-off process. You should avoid omitting it or even take the matters into your own hands. The way out of this predicament is to discuss the issue with the powers that be on the customer side. Management on the customer side has to solve anything causing friction on their side. In harmless cases, a person's vacation without an adequate substitute may be the cause. I've experienced it more than once that management stepped in and helped to provide the sign-off themselves. Just don't allow yourselves to be blocked.

10.11. Communication

In the last section, I discussed how a clear concept of ownership drives your communication regarding the flow of changes to the productive system, which is owned by the customer. Only when a unit of work is used in production, it will create value for the customer. Until then, it is just work in progress.

Clear communication is important for every other aspect of your contract work. When you provide operations support, you also need to communicate the state of affairs when you need to resolve an operational issue. Ideally, you know of production issues before your customer does and can inform him about the problem and that you are already in the process of resolving the issue.

Handling stuff proactively helps to build trust. Don't be a black box, but make your work as transparent as possible by practicing good communication and informing everyone who needs to know.

What about other contractors involved in the project? Too much communication can be overkill. When working on largely independent deliverables, the responsible parties should act as autonomously as possible. When working on the same deliverable, you should strive to integrate them into an organization-spanning meta-team where everybody is in the loop about what is going on.

10.12. Diligence

We are humans and we like to take shortcuts. Don't. Rather be diligent. Don't omit quality gates to speed up your process, e.g., by promoting a release even if some unit tests fail. This could mean putting a release on production that hasn't been properly acceptance tested. Don't omit code reviews, even when there is no reviewer available.

As a last resort, switch your hat from developer to reviewer and perform that step yourself. Explain a concept to a rubber duck if there is no real person available. Don't assume it will work without proper diligence. Stupid mistakes will happen if you are negligent. Poka Yoke is all about avoiding stupid mistakes by taking precautions to prevent them from happening.

The next chapter contains some experience of what happens if you do not take every care you can to eliminate mistakes. Go the extra mile to verify by yourself that everything is well. The best monitoring system can put you in a false sense of security by not sounding an alert. Human diligence is still not replaceable by automation.

When you need to integrate with services from other organizations, make sure you couple to them as loosely as possible with as few assumptions about availability, performance or correctness as possible. Be sure you can answer all questions about what happens on hand-over points to be able to fix issues when they are on your side or to limit damage and have them fixed by the other side if you find that the issue is with the other party. When you work with subcontractors contributing to your delivery, make sure that they are as diligent as you are, or compensate by taking extra care that you get the quality you need.

10.13. Clear responsibility

It is not sufficient to know that something has to be done. There is no better way to muddy responsibilities than pulling as many people into a meeting and noting that somebody has to take action. When it is 'somebody', nobody will feel responsible. Therefore, you need to make sure who is responsible to take some action. The responsible person has the option to delegate, but still needs to make sure that the intended result is actually achieved.

When several contractors work on a single delivery, the question of who is responsible gets really important. Often, it is resolved by having a main contractor who subcontracts parts of the whole delivery. It might be OK to task several independent service providers when you need to evaluate someone else's work. Again, an analogy with good medical practice is helpful. You might want to have a separate contract to ask for an independent second opinion, but you should not have several physicians treating you for the same illness at the same time. In the next part, I will relate some experiences where a customer did exactly that. The result was chaotic, and you might classify the culture of the customer as pathological with respect to the Westrum typology.

11. Evolution in Service Organizations by Example

Cultural aspects are surely much more difficult to assess in a project situation where several contractors are involved. Each contractor brings its own culture to the table, and it is a challenge to find a common denominator to work together. This might be the reason why DevOps research comes to the conclusion that "DevOps works best for in-house projects". Remember this assessment? I want to describe my experience with a selection of projects I was involved with. I describe the general setup of the involved parties, project management styles and cultural clashes or alignment. I will try to put everything into context of my values from the last chapter. All projects share one commonality: The goal was to establish a web shop. The web shop had to be integrated with some enterprise software of the customer and some external services.

11.1. Web Shop for a Dealership

The first project was for a dealership where not only the own products of the dealership were sold, but which also included third-party sales, which made processing of orders more complex. The web shop provider wasn't the primary contractor in this case, but nevertheless took over a lot of project management responsibility, like providing forecasts and milestone plans and organizing phone conferences between all contractors involved and the dealership. Without going above and beyond the duty of a subcontractor, the whole project might have never gone live.

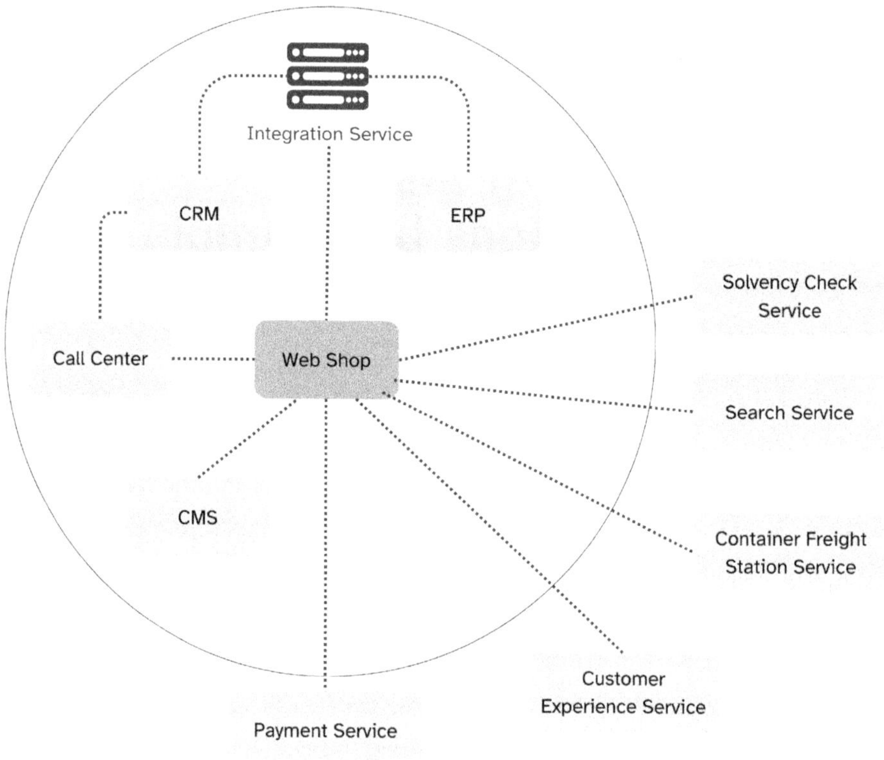

Figure 11.1.: System Integration Diagram Dealer, Web Shop Perspective

11.1.1. Project Setup

A customer relationship management system (CRM) could be regarded as the main component of the system. The provider of this system was the main contractor. Central to the system was a data integration server which was customized by a data integration specialist who was responsible for pushing the product catalog into the web shop and pulling the orders from the web shop and splitting them into parts for the different third-party providers to do drop delivery.

Payments were handled by a payment service provider with no prior e-commerce experience. There was a certified integration with the web shop available from a third party. This dictated the selection of the version of the web shop base version which wasn't the latest, but the one for which the payment solution integration was available and certified.

The hosting provider was chosen by the dealership and had no experience with the chosen web shop software. Therefore, very detailed information how to set up the database and load balancing for the application front-ends and other infrastructure topics like machine sizing and service configuration was needed. The dealer had high requirements for the availability and integrity of the e-commerce system.

A content management system was also integrated with the web shop. The purpose was to provide themed areas to present products related to a given theme to further cross-selling. The customization was done by a specialized subcontractor who pushed his contributions to a dedicated integration branch of the web shop provider, who then integrated it on his main branch.

An important part was integration with a support front-end for call center agents who needed to be able to research orders and their status and also be able to act on the end customer's behalf to place, change or cancel orders. The call center was a dedicated web shop instance and completely decoupled from the web shop developments for the end customers.

To help end customers find products, a search engine was also integrated with the web shop. Another web shop specialist was chosen by the dealer to do this integration.

Further services that were integrated with support by special providers include a customer experience solution, delivery to container freight stations and a credit check which enabled 'unsafe' payment methods only for customers with a good credit rating. For an overview of the system landscape, see figure 11.1.

This overview is shown from the perspective of the web shop provider, who, of course, takes the liberty to put himself at the center of the universe.

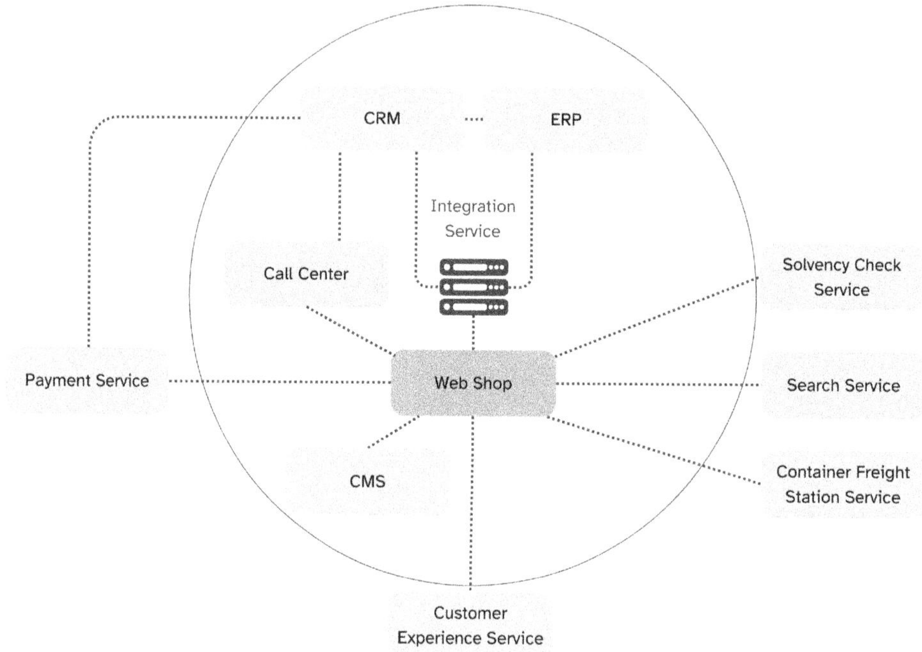

Figure 11.2.: System Integration Diagram Dealer, CRM Perspective

For completeness's sake, I show the view of the CRM provider (see figure 11.2, which had the integration service as the central component and which shows a few additional connections from the CRM to the payment provider (for capturing credit card payments) and to the ERP system. Those connections were basically 'invisible' from the perspective of the web shop.

11.1.2. Project Evaluation

Regarding the Westrum cultural typology, the project could be classified as being steered by a pathological organization. There wasn't too much trust between the dealership and its contractors, which probably also was due to a choleric boss at the dealership who tried to manage the project with power and pressure. He even belittled his own employees in an on-site workshop with all service providers.

When you look at the meta organization, which consists of all stakeholders in the project, you probably also have to judge it as pathological. All contractors were direct contractors of the dealership. There was no subcontracting, which might have improved the steering. Nevertheless, the contractors did their best to bring some kind of structure into the project.

A big mistake in the development of this system was to provide sample products in the shop so that some tests could already be done before the product catalog import was fully implemented. This had a double disadvantage: The sample products were scraped from the web shop of another dealership. Of course, the mood of the dealership did not improve with every additional week they had to test with the products of a competitor!

There was no automatic deployment. Deployment was a manual process which took roughly one day to install a new version of the customized web shop software and its configuration. Since it was such an arduous and lengthy process, deployments were done at most monthly.

In principle, there were systems for integration tests, acceptance test and production, but they weren't really used according to this purpose. The acceptance test system was described as the playground for the business and the integration system as the playground for development. Since there was only one test instance of the ERP system, it had to be switched between the two web shop test instances.

There was no concept of quality gates which had to be passed when code was promoted forward. There even wasn't a clear concept of promotion. Some contractors did not work with the version control system, but performed their integration work on the servers themselves.

Of course, there could be no reliability or reproducibility in this way. But the corresponding mentality is perhaps best illustrated by the quote "we are now working on the live system, the staging system is not relevant anymore". In the end, the project went successfully live, but of course, there is no sustainability with such a working mode.

With such a working mode, you put a system live and then someday you start a relaunch project to build a new system and (hopefully) migrate to the new system and put it live. There is basically little chance to efficiently react to changing requirements. Delivery performance was low in this project.

The pain associated with a deployment was so high, that it happened at most once every other month during the development phase. Of course, after the project went live, reluctance for deployment was even higher. It was always risky to put something productive which couldn't be sensibly tested in advance.

When it went live, the project did add value to the dealership, but it wasn't sustainable. The dealer eventually relaunched his e-commerce system based on a different platform. There was no overall vision for the whole project that was shared by all stakeholders.

Transparency wasn't high since there was no continuous delivery capability. The dealership could only see what has been developed when one of the infrequent deployments happened. Even worse, there wasn't even transparency for the web shop component for the web shop contractor, since the dealership tasked another contractor with the integration of a search engine.

This resulted in a version conflict, since the chosen integration was for a newer version of the web shop platform (we chose not to use the latest version because the payment integration wasn't available for it).

All in all, trust wasn't high and the division lead on the side of the dealership didn't treat the contractors well (neither did he treat his own employees with respect and trust). There were micro discussions about the invoiced effort to get back some of the money spent. Many workers in the project were unable to keep their morale up.

Ownership of the systems was unclear. Of course, in the end the dealership owned everything, but it was in part unclear who did what on which system. There was no clear quality process and the deliveries were only

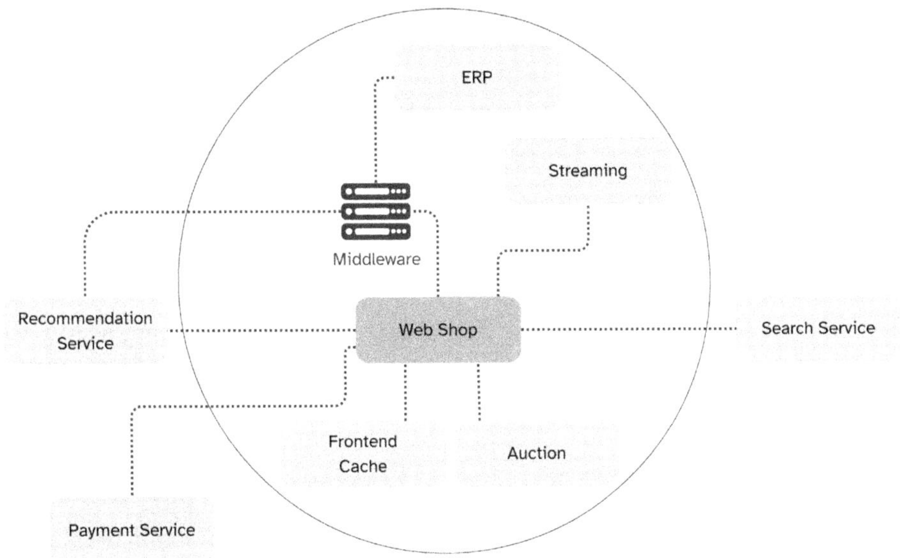

Figure 11.3.: System Integration Diagram Auctioneer

roughly defined as a list of implemented features without full transparency into the exact changes and their relation to the requirements from the dealership.

11.2. Web Shop for an Auction Platform

Our second example is a web shop for an auction platform. In this case, the web shop provider was the main contractor for the project. A special requirement was to extend the web shop with auction capabilities. A further special feature was the capability for A/B testing to compare cart abandonment rates, e.g., when additional incentives were added to the shopping cart vs. the case when this was not done.

11.2.1. Project Setup

The auction company already had a middleware that served for the integration with their enterprise platform. The web shop still needed to be customized (especially to provide auction capabilities) and integrated with the ERP system and some external services. The integration with the ERP served to get product catalog data into the web shop and orders back into the ERP system. In front of the web shop, a front-end caching server was used to improve response times and reduce load on the transaction processing server.

Integration with a payment service provider is just about standard for every web shop solution. Another standard service was a full-text search engine. A special service in this project was a recommendation service which was used to calculate shopping cart abandonment probability. This was used to lower the abandonment of carts by providing extra incentives. More special integration tasks were a streaming service for live videos and the auction service which used video for live auctions. An overview of the system landscape is shown in figure 11.3.

11.2.2. Project Evaluation

I would put the culture of this project's organization according to the Westrum typology somewhere between pathological and bureaucratic. The capability to deliver was quite a bit better than with the previous example. The team had created a deployment script which got deployment times down to minutes. Of course, reproducibility was much better in this way.

The capability to do automatic deployments didn't result in high trust, however. Besides the production system, there was an acceptance test and an integration system, but they were not used to create a delivery pipeline with quality gates.

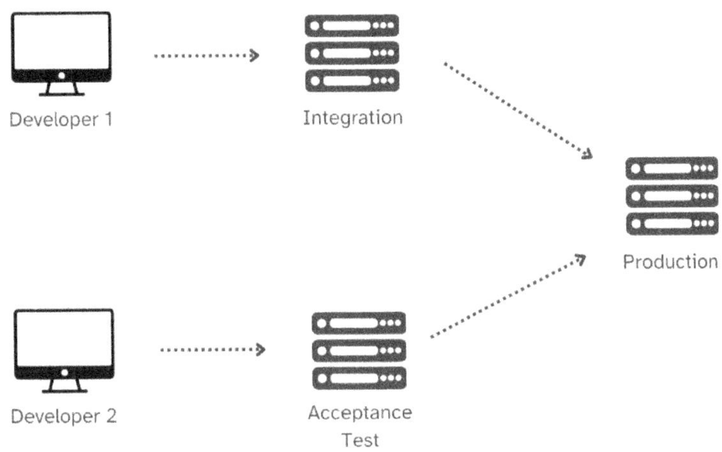

Figure 11.4.: Delivery Process, Broken Quality Assurance

Instead, the auctioneer had the idea that the two systems could be used to test drive two feature development branches at the same time. Production deployment was done in a bureaucratic way (once per week, ready or not, here we come!) and it was driven by the wish of the auctioneer to have one of the features tested on either the acceptance test or integration system available on production. The corresponding delivery process is shown in figure 11.4.

You can immediately see that you will lose at least one quality gate in this way. Even worse, it was not well understood neither by the customer nor by the development team that changes will be missing, that were not merged on the feature branch currently being deployed. The deployment worked as implemented, but it was probably imagined that a feature that had just been tested would be added to what was running on production. Without properly merging a feature branch to some mainline branch!

The result was that in about half of those weekly deployment feasts, the production system had to be rolled back quickly. Very soon after the deployment was done, it was noted that something was not behaving as it should.

Testability outside the production system was limited. A developer of the web shop team claimed that the deployment process had to be fast for two reasons: He wanted to be able to roll back quickly when something unexpected happened, and he wanted to get changes quickly into production to be able to test them there.

There seemed to be no concept of a highly available live system nor a quantitative idea of a monthly error budget to even stop making changes when this error budget is used up. To achieve high availability, you, of course, need to do everything you can to have everything tested before it goes live and therefore be very confident that nothing unexpected happens.

When I helped out in this project, I was tasked to work on the integration of the recommendation service. To my utter shock, it was only accessible from the production system! You could not test the integration with this external service without putting your code changes on production!

Therefore, my first action was to establish testability of the recommendation service. Once I got the necessary whitelisting in the firewall of the provider of this service, the sandbox version for this service still did not respond. It wasn't up and running, since nobody had ever used it.

To add insult to injury, once the service was running, it did not provide the proper service as booked by the auctioneer, since it didn't have the same modules installed that were available on the production service. The lesson from this is: When you can't test something on your development machine, on the integration or user acceptance system, you have to establish testability. Otherwise, you are flying blind.

I think all this shows enough cause for the auctioneer to not put trust into the development process. It wasn't very transparent, he could only rely on regular destructive deployments on his live system. Ownership of the production system wasn't really respected since the auctioneer never really knew what he would get (just like Forrest Gump, who said: “My mom always said life was like a box of chocolates. You never know what you’re gonna get.”).

But there was nobody who could really tell him. There were no release notes that documented what would change. It would not have been possible to provide such release notes truthfully, since often it was one step forward and at the same time two steps backwards. The lesson to take from this is to always implement a strict forward process (for an explanation of the term “strict forward process”, see section 10.2).

11.3. Web Shop for a Manufacturer

The third example is a web shop for a large manufacturer which is used for worldwide distribution of his service goods. The web shop provider was the main contractor who subcontracted development work and infrastructure support.

11.3.1. Project Setup

There was a self-hosted search service based on ElasticSearch and the web shop had to be integrated not only with the ERP and the single-sign-on solution of the manufacturer, but also with an internal license service, since some products required software licenses to be operated. Figure 11.5 shows an overview of the completely self-hosted system.

11.3.2. Project Evaluation

The culture in this project was close to a generative culture. The delivery capability was pretty good. It was possible and also sometimes necessary to execute close to 10 deploys per day. The reliability of the delivery process

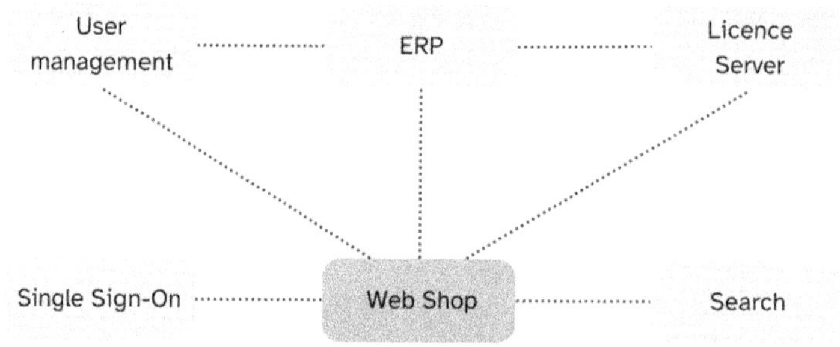

Figure 11.5.: System Integration Diagram Manufacturer

was very high, the error rate when going to production was close to zero. This was achieved by following a strict forward process, as shown in figure 10.1.

Each stage in the delivery process was handled as a strict quality gate. The developers worked on small, short-lived feature branches that were merged to the main line after a four-eye code review. There weren't many automatic tests, but there was a strict rule that all changes, that were automatically deployed on the integration system, had to be checked to be working as expected.

A set of verified changes were deployed to the acceptance test system after all changes had been confirmed to be working on the integration system. The deployment on the acceptance test system was accompanied by detailed release notes that provided full transparency into what was changed on the acceptance test system, which was considered to be owned by the manufacturer (as well as, of course, the production system).

Those changes were only promoted to production once the manufacturer had signed them off. The testing in the acceptance test system was done thoroughly by a special division, which also automated their tests as much as possible. In this way, surprises when going productive were extremely rare. A rollback never needed to be executed.

Communication in the overall project organization was very open, honest, and proactive. There was a very clear understanding who owned which part of the system, and the rule that no planned changes were applied to the manufacturer's system without their knowledge and informed consent was obeyed strictly.

Business feedback was provided on several levels. There were regular retrospectives and also more informal exchanges between "power users" and developers. This feedback was direct with no intermediaries, so misunderstandings could be clarified immediately in most cases. My impression was that the resulting level of trust was very high.

The very good level of business feedback wasn't there from day one, however. It took a large effort to establish it. The first big hurdle was to set up integration, acceptance test and production environment in a zero trust environment, which took a long time to set up, since IT operations were sourced out and handled in a very bureaucratic way. To get started, we set up a test environment with our own operations people (this took a few days, including automatic deployment and an initial version of the application). This allowed us to close the feedback loop with the business people, even while we were still struggling with setting up the system in their own data center.

12. Closing Remarks

This part about cultural aspects can be viewed as an attempt to get a glimpse at the bigger picture from down in the trenches. Not a bird's-eye view from a management perspective and not the expert view of a sociologist, but the observations of a curious software practitioner on his journey towards some craftsmanship in his profession. More important than a perfect specification is getting something usable into the hands of your customer as soon as possible. And usable does not mean a prototype or a proof of concept, but rather something like a minimum viable product which can be grown into a fuller solution incrementally. Only in this way you will be able to check the validity of your work.

Often I observe the following: A system is built which is completed and then put into operation. The servers in this system are set up with the necessary services. Some custom software is developed and put on one or more of those servers. Then a big switch is flipped, and the whole thing is put live in some kind of big bang event.

Often, it really is a big bang but also a big silence afterward, since what has been built isn't up to its task. Or if it is initially, it quickly gets outdated and the need to build a new system arises. In my view, it is much better to implement a process by which you can continuously deliver value for your customer. Chances are that you will be able to satisfy your customer's need much better and in a more sustainable way.

An integral part of this process is getting feedback from your customer as soon as possible. You will often notice that you did not foresee some aspect that is essential for your customer. You will only find out by delivering a usable implementation early and having the business people scrutinize it.

It can be very hard to close this feedback loop with the customer, but it is totally worth the effort. Plus, this effort has to be spent continuously to keep this feedback loop going.

The three example cases show progressively better results regarding customer satisfaction and the capability to deliver changes to production quickly without hampering the availability and the integrity of the production system. This contributes substantially to building trust, which, in turn, I think is essential for achieving this outcome. It looks like a hen and egg problem. But, in reality, it isn't.

Don't hide from your customer after you did a requirement analysis phase and then an implementation phase with no contact with your customer like it is advocated by waterfall type methods where testing happens at the end of the development phase. Invest extra effort to close the feedback loop with your customer.

Include the customer on every step of the way. It is very likely that the business people will be glad to be part of the full process and part of a larger team. Of course, you can rarely do team building exercises in a contract relationship. You have more formal encounters like workshops and reviews. A good way to strengthen the relationship is to have some less formal encounters where you improve your understanding of the requirements and common testing sessions. Being open-minded on both contractor and on client side will help a lot to find a common mode of working together. Both parties should not try to force a working mode on the other party but look for ways to communicate fast and directly with preferably no intermediaries.

It will help not to put blame on anybody, but to clarify what is needed. Delivering a fix for an issue while it is being discussed also helps a lot to build trust and common understanding. The idea of DevOps to break down the barrier between development and operations also applies to the wall between business and development. The hurdle can be much larger, but it can be overcome when both sides want to work together.

Success is less a question of technology and far more a question of working together and not against each other. Uncompromising transparency and honesty are essential. Otherwise, the different parties in a project lack information to adapt their internal planning, which results in friction loss and unnecessary blocking. This can slow down a project to the point that it is effectively dead.

Do I think that we have reached the end of our journey towards delivering better software and in a more efficient way? I don't think so. I think we can keep improving and that there will be improved ways to build, deliver, and operate software. I also think that AI might be an integral part of our tool chain, but we shouldn't expect it to take over our job anytime soon. There is simply too much understanding, culture and honesty involved.

List of Figures

2.1 System integration diagram 13
2.2 System integration diagram publisher (simple) 15
2.3 System integration diagram publisher (complex) 16
2.4 System operation diagram 19

4.1 Process diagram 34

5.1 The State of Affairs 49

6.1 Overflowing Message Queue 76
6.2 Professor Butts and the Self-Operating Napkin by Rube Goldberg (1933) 77
6.3 Flexibility as Source of Errors 82
6.4 Simple Control-Flow 98
6.5 Operation Responsibility Graph 104
6.6 The Hare and the Hedgehog by Otto Ubbelohde (1909) . . 109

7.1 DevOps Beyond In-house 114

10.1 Delivery Process 125
10.2 Delivery Process Feedback 126
10.3 Cumulative Quality Assurance 127
10.4 Multiple Service Providers 135

11.1 System Integration Diagram Dealer, Web Shop Perspective 140
11.2 System Integration Diagram Dealer, CRM Perspective . . . 142
11.3 System Integration Diagram Auctioneer 145
11.4 Delivery Process, Broken Quality Assurance 147

11.5 System Integration Diagram Manufacturer 150

List of Tables

2.1 Data Flows 14

4.1 North American Regions 28
4.2 Nordics Regions 29

5.1 Content of Table User 55
5.2 Content of Table Address 55
5.3 Addresses of User 'a' 57
5.4 Output of `EXPLAIN` 57
5.5 Output of `EXPLAIN` (optimized) 58

8.1 Software Delivery Performance for 2016 117
8.2 Software Delivery Performance for 2017 117

Listings

4.1 Apple's SSL/TLS Bug 33

5.1 Create user and address tables 54
5.2 Ill performing SELECT 56
5.3 `EXPLAIN` query plan for `SELECT` 57
5.4 Add missing index 58

6.1 Flawed search indexer 80
6.2 Usage of flawed search indexer 81
6.3 Immutable search indexer 84
6.4 Usage of the immutable search indexer 85
6.5 DataTransfer class 86
6.6 Usage of the DataTransfer class 87
6.7 Usage of better DataTransfer class 88
6.8 Ill performing variant selector code 91
6.9 Better performing variant selector code 92
6.10 Display location with weather 93
6.11 Simple branching code example 98

Bibliography

Agile-Ideation (2023). *Westrum Organizational Culture Model Unveiled: Your Guide to Generative Culture, Cultural Typologies, and Psychological Safety.* URL: https://agile-ideation.com/blog/2023/8/9/westrum-organizational-culture-model-unveiled-your-guide-to-generative-culture-cultural-typologies-and-psychological-safety (visited on 03/24/2024).

Allspaw, John and Paul Hammond (2009). *10+ Deploys per Day: Dev and Ops Cooperation at Flickr.* URL: https://www.slideshare.net/jallspaw/10-deploys-per-day-dev-and-ops-cooperation-at-flickr (visited on 08/12/2023).

Apple (2024). *sslKeyExchange.* URL: https://opensource.apple.com/source/Security/Security-55471/libsecurity_ssl/lib/sslKeyExchange.c (visited on 07/26/2024).

Beyer, Betsy et al. (2016). *Site Reliability Engineering.* O'Reilly.

Bryar, Colin and Bill Carr (2021). *working backward.* St. Martin's Press.

Cyclomatic complexity (2023). URL: https://en.wikipedia.org/wiki/Cyclomatic_complexity (visited on 03/02/2023).

Feathers, Michael C. (2009). *Working Effectively with Legacy Code.* Pearson Education.

Forsgren, Nicole, Jim Humble, and Gene Kim (2018). *Accelerate.* IT Revolution.

Istio Service Mesh (2023). URL: https://istio.io/ (visited on 03/07/2023).

Jaeger: open source, distributed tracing platform (2023). URL: https://www.jaegertracing.io/ (visited on 03/07/2023).

Kim, Gene, Kevin Behr, and George Spafford (2014). *The Phoenix Project.* IT Revolution Press.

Knight, Will (2024). *The AI-Powered Future of Coding Is Near.* URL: https://www.wired.com/ai-powered-coding/ (visited on 07/18/2024).

Langley, Adam (2024). *sslKeyExchange.* URL: https://opensource.apple.com/source/Security/Security-55471/libsecurity_ssl/lib/sslKeyExchange.c (visited on 07/26/2024).

Majors, Charity, Liz Fong-Jones, and George Miranda (2022). O'Reilly Media.

Martin, Robert C (2009). *Clean Code: A Handbook of Agile Software Crafstmanship.* Pearson Education.

Nygard, Michael T. (2018). *Release It! Second Edition.* The Pragmatic Programmers.

Sites, Richard L. (2022). *Understanding Software Dynamics.* Pearson Education.

Spolsky, Joel (2000). *Things You Should Never Do, Part I.* URL: https://www.joelonsoftware.com/2000/04/06/things-you-should-never-do-part-i/ (visited on 03/02/2023).

— (2004). *Joel on Software.* apress.

Tornhill, Adam (2018). *Software Design X-Rays.* The Pragmatic Programmers.

Van Roy, Peter (2024). *Programming Paradigms for Dummies: What Every Programmer Should Know.* URL: https://webperso.info.ucl.ac.be/~pvr/VanRoyChapter.pdf (visited on 08/02/2024).

Winters, Titus, Tom Manshreck, and Hyrum Wright (2020). *Software Engineering at Google.* O'Reilly Media.

Index

10+ deploys per day, 124

A/B testing, 145
abstract class, 74
Accelerate, 113, 115, 119, 120
acceptance test, 5, 7, 35, 42, 50, 68, 127, 131, 133, 134, 137, 143
acceptance test environment, 5
acceptance test system, 127, 133, 134, 143, 146, 147, 150, 151
accounting system, 13
Adam Tornhill, 100
agile, 8, 23, 66
agility, 120
AI, xi
Albert Einstein, 70, 85
algorithms, 23
alienation, 7, 24
always check your assumptions, 69
Amazon, 121
analysis, 48
analyzability, 96
Andon cord, 66
anti-pattern, 79, 81, 82
Apache, 115
API, 30, 31, 84, 85, 87, 89, 121
Apple, 32, 107
Apple II, 108
application server, 93, 94

apprentice, 21, 120
asset management system, 13
at-most-once, 90
automatic delivery process, 5
automatic deployment, 116, 143, 146
automatic test, 125
availability, 42, 137, 141
awareness, 27, 30

banking application, 13
batch job, 17, 51
batch process, 38, 101
Behavior, 82
Bertrand Meyer, 30
best practice, 23, 132
Bill Carr, 121
binlog, 46
blameless postmortem, 59
blue/green deployment, 36
boy scouts rule, 9, 72
build, 5, 66, 133
Bulkhead, 95
bureaucratic, 119, 120, 132, 146, 147, 151
bureaucratic culture, 119, 132
business
    feedback, 40, 41, 43, 151, 153
    logic, 20, 35
    owner, 121, 135
    ownership, 122
    requirement, 11, 42, 43

C, 59
C++, 24, 59
call center, 141

callback, 88
capability to deliver, 124, 144, 146, 149, 154
cart abandonment rate, 145
challenging fate, 81
change failure rate, 115
circuit breaker, 95
city, 30
clean code, 73
cloud, 36, 104, 105
cloud management system, 104
cluster analysis, 115
CMS, 135
code review, 5, 126, 137, 150
code scanner, 125
coding, xi
Colin Bryar, 121
common understanding, 154
communication, 19, 131, 132, 136, 151
compensating transaction, 90
complexity, 74–76, 78, 88
computability, 23
computer science, 23
configuration changes, 124
connection pool, 91
consistency, 78, 89
constraint, 69, 71, 79
container freight station, 141
content management system, 75, 135, 141
continuous improvcmcnt, 7, 8, 69, 119, 120
contract project, 113, 116, 117, 120, 123, 131, 134
contract relationship, 154
contracting entity, 113
control.flow graph, 99

Conway's law, 19
coolness, 73
correctness, 137
CPU, 8, 30, 37, 46, 90, 92, 94
craftsmanship, 153
creativity, 120
credit check, 141
credit rating, 141
CRM, 135, 140, 142
cultural transformation, 113
cultural typology, 114, 142
cultural values, 114
culture of learning, 119
customer orientation, 11
customer relationship management system, 135, 140
customer satisfaction, 154
cyclomatic complexity, 97, 99

damage control, 72, 95, 106, 137
data flow, 12–17, 41
data structure, 23, 86
database, 94
    connection, 37, 46, 51, 77, 90
    connection pool, 39
    schema, 47, 54
    schema change, 28, 36, 124
    server, 90, 92
    theory, 23
DB2, 56
deadline, 131–133
dealership, 139
debug, 74, 116
debugger, 74

definition of done, 5
delivery cost, 27, 28
delivery pipeline, 49, 116, 122, 124, 128, 130, 146
delivery process, 5, 133, 149, 150
deployment fear, 115, 124
deployment frequency, 115
deployment pain, 144
Design by Contract, 30
development environment, 23, 116
development process, 19, 148
DevOps, 3, 4, 7, 8, 11, 12, 18, 30, 65, 71, 107, 113–120, 123, 124, 130, 139, 154
    engineer, 3, 4, 120
    first pillar of, 4, 42, 119
    second pillar of, 7, 30, 119, 124
    third pillar of, 69, 119
diligence, 137
dishwasher, 78
disk space, 90
distributed architecture, 102
distributed system, 106, 107
distributed tracing, 103
documentation tool, 24
don't waste resources, 90
Doxygen, 25
drop delivery, 140
DRY, 82
dryer, 78
dysfunctional object, 79

e-commerce, 90, 140, 141, 144
eBook delivery system, 16
edge case, 96

Eiffel, 30
ElasticSearch, 149
Elixir, 31
emergency switch, 95
engineering, xi
enterprise resource planning system, *see also* ERP, 41
enterprise software, 12
enterprise system, 12
Erlang, 20, 31
Erlang/OTP, 82
ERP, *see also* enterprise resource planning system, 105, 106, 143, 146, 149
error budget, 18, 148
error rate, 150
eventually consistent, 76
executable requirement, 134
expectable behavior, 68, 83
EXPLAIN, 56, 57
extensibility, 73
external service, 101

Fail Fast, 95
feature, 97
feature branch, 24, 67, 147, 150
feature toggle, 42, 68
federal state, 27
feedback, 7, 30–32, 67, 119, 122, 130, 133, 134, 151
feedback loop, 7, 40–43, 114, 151, 154
firewall, 148
first in, first out, 78
first of all, do no harm, 130
flexibility, 78, 81, 100
flight booking system, 27
Flow, 4, 41, 42, 72, 114, 119, 124

Forrest Gump, 149
framework, 68, 82
front-end caching, 146
full table scan, 51, 56, 57

garbage collection, 59, 92
Gene Kim, 4, 113
generative, 120
generative culture, 120, 133, 149
George Spafford, 4
good medical practice, 129, 130, 134, 138
Google, 126
greenfield, 9, 12, 28, 29, 107–110

Handshaking, 95
happy path, 20, 32, 38, 88, 106
hare and hedgehog, 109
high availability, 148
high performance cluster, 115
high-performance organization, 113, 115
highly scalable systems, 96
Hollywood principle, 82
honesty, 131, 132, 155
horizontal scaling, 6
HTTP, 107
HTTPS, 105

IBM, 56
idempotency, 89, 90
ignorance, 23
immutability, 100
immutable, 81
immutable indexer, 83
in-house, 117

in-house developer, 116
in-house development, 116, 123, 130
in-house project, 113, 114, 118, 120, 139
incident, 105, 106
inconsistent state, 47
indentation, 97
index, 51
Indexer, 79
informed consent, 122, 128, 134, 151
informed decision, 122
infrastructure, 104, 105
infrastructure as code, 6
integration environment, 5
integration system, 127, 129
integration test, 32, 34
integrity, 141
interactive system, 17
interface, 24, 73, 74, 84–86, 88
inversion-of-control, 82
ISO 3166-2, 28
Istio, 96, 103

Jaeger, 103
Jim Humble, 113
job satisfaction, 119
Joel Spolsky, 96, 107
John Allspaw, 124
journeyman, 120
JSON, 52

Kaizen, 69
Kanban, 67, 72, 77
Kevin Behr, 4
kill the messenger, 132

knowledge sharing, 60
KUTrace, 103

last in, first out, 78
latency, 75, 78, 93, 95
lead developer, 43
lead time, 115
Lean, 65, 67, 71
learning, 120
legacy, 107–110
legacy code, 96
legacy software, 9
Let it Crash, 20, 95
library, 85, 96
limit damage, 93
limit work in progress, 72
Linus Torvalds, 97
Linux, 97, 103
Lisa, 108
Little's Law, 67, 77
load balancer, 105
load test, 35
load test environment, 5
load test system, 36
log file, 18, 51
log level, 38, 52, 101, 102
logfile analysis, 51
logging, 38–40, 50–52, 101, 102
logging level, 102
loose coupling, 88

Macintosh, 107
main contractor, 145, 149
maintainability, 108

maintenance phase, 83
management buy-in, 121
market data system, 13
master/slave replication, 46, 47
McCabe, 99
mean time to recovery, 115
memory, 90, 92
memory leak, 20, 59
memory profiling, 58, 59
message queue, 75, 89
Michael Nygard, 95
microservice, 102, 121
microservice architecture, 70, 121
middleware, 74, 104–107, 146
minimum viable product, 11, 71
mitigation, 45
modesty, 132
monitoring, 37, 40, 50, 102, 105, 106, 137
MTTR, 115
Muda, 69, 78
multi-pass processing, 75
Multiple Service Providers, 135
Murphy's law, 20

nested call graphs, 40
Netscape, 96, 107
network bandwith, 90
network connection, 90
never consistent, 76
Niklaus Wirth, xi, 71
Nils Forsgren, 113
non-determinism, 82
NoSQL, 53

not my business, 107

OAuth, 32
observability, 40, 48, 50, 101
observability engineering, 40, 103
open heart surgery, 116
operability, 18, 73
operation responsibility graph, 105
operational issue, 136
operations, 17
operations issues, 17
operator, 17
optimizer, 54
organizational culture, 118–120
Overflowing Message Queue, 76
ownership, 134, 148

pathological, 120
pathological culture, 119
Paul Hammond, 124
payment service, 140
payment service provider, 146
PEN test, 36, 37
PEN test environment, 5
performance, 47, 50, 52, 73, 75, 97, 109, 137
performance schema, 58
Poka Yoke, 68, 83, 137
power, 119
power user, 151
preparedness, 65, 132
primary contractor, 139
processing time, 92
product information system, 41
product management system, 16, 91

product owner, 43, 121
product variant, 91
productive system, 134, 136
Professor Butts, 77
profiling, 50, 52, 53
programming, xi
programming language, 23, 24, 30, 68, 96
project management, 23
project manager, 43
proof of concept, 83
Protobuf, 52
protocol, 86, 87, 93
psychological safety, 120
purpose, 85, 99
push one button, 116

quality, 125
quality assurance, 126, 129
quality gate, 5, 66, 67, 126, 127, 129, 131, 137, 143, 146, 150
quality process, 144
query plan, 53, 54, 57, 58
queuing, 40, 88

RDMBS, 53
reactivity, 45
readability, 52, 108, 126
recommendation service, 146, 148
refactoring, 100
region, 27, 28
regression test, 49, 50
Relational Database Management System, 53
relaunch, 144
release early, release often, 67
release notes, 131, 134, 149, 150

reliability, 143, 149
remote call, 101
remote service, 85, 94
repairability, 73
reporting, 39
reproducibility, 143, 146
requirement, 100
requirement management system, 100, 134
resource consumption, 93
resource pool, 51
responsibility, 18, 59, 107, 138
REST, 52
retrospective, 151
ring replication, 47
risk, 120
robust code, 82
robustness, 20, 52, 73, 79, 82, 97, 103
rollback, 150
Ron Westrum, 114, 118, 119, 142
Rube Goldberg, 77
Rube Goldberg machine, 77
run-time, 96

sales tax, 27
sandbox, 148
Scrum, 5, 23, 67, 121
search engine, 141, 144, 146
search service, 79, 149
security scan, 130
segregation of concerns, 79
self-operating napkin, 77
service level indicator, 37
service level objective, 30, 37

service mesh, 96, 103
SIGHUP, 115
sign-off, 125, 134, 135
silent mail, 131
silo, 4
silver bullet, 113
simplicity, 85
single purpose team, 121
single-sign-on, 149
site reliability engineering, 18, 59
SLI, 102
SLO, 102
slow query, 50, 58
software delivery performance, 115, 117, 120, 144
software delivery pipeline, 66–70, 72, 128
software delivery process, 125, 126
software deployment pipeline, 41
Software Design X-Rays, 100
software development methodology, 23
software engineer, 77
software metric, 97
SOLID, 99
source code management, 23
SSH, 105
stability, 109
stability patterns, 95
stack, 31
stack frame, 92
Steady State, 95
streaming, 89
streaming service, 146
strict forward process, 128, 149, 150
strict typing, 125

sub-contractor, 139, 141
subscription management system, 16
Sun Tzu, 68
sustainability, 143, 153
system analysis, 12
system context diagram, 14
system diagram, 18
system integration, 12
system integration diagram, 14

template method, 82
The Art of War, 68
The Phoenix Project, 4
the right way, 130
thread pool, 39
time to first byte, 38
time to market, 120
timeout, 94, 95, 107
Toyota, 65
tracing, 50
transaction, 89, 90
transaction unit, 78
transparency, 122, 131, 144, 145, 148, 150, 155
trunk-based development, 129
trust, 119, 120, 131–133, 146, 148, 151, 154
Turing machine, 23

unhappy path, 20, 32, 39, 88, 106
unique constraint, 47
unit test, 5, 24, 30, 31
UNIX, 115
user experience, 84

vacation booking application, 93

value for the customer, 5, 17, 24, 27, 30, 41, 43, 66, 71, 72, 119, 122, 129, 130, 136, 153
variant selector, 91
version control, 24, 43, 100
version control system, 43, 143
vertical scaling, 6
virtual memory, 58
visibility, 101
vision, 130, 144
visionary leadership, 121

waterfall method, 8, 154
weather condition, 93
weather data, 93, 95
weather service, 93–95
web service, 32, 52
web shop, 16, 35, 41, 45, 75, 91, 104–107, 116, 140, 141, 143, 145, 146, 149
web worker, 94, 95
Westrum typology, 120, 138, 146
work in progress, 43, 136
worker, 76
working backwards, 121
wrong assumptions, 27, 51, 101

XML, 52, 75

YAGNI, 130
You Ain't Gonna Need It, 130

Zalando, 121
zero trust, 151
ZIP code, 30

Acknowledgments

First, I want to thank Tosca Schuhmacher. When I started the book while visiting her parent's place in Italy, she saw the first pages I wrote and took an immediate interest in the project. Maybe some day, she will write a book of her own.

The most important contributor to the project is Prof. Walter Kriha. He read it several times in various stages and offered extensive suggestions for improvements. I have known Walter since 1994, and we worked together on several occasions in advanced software projects. I also had the opportunity to hold a talk on Elixir at one of his language days at the Hochschule der Medien in Stuttgart.

Caroline Helbing helped to polish the book to make it ready for production. She took care of proofreading, making the graphic elements beautiful and clear and making the layout decent. She also took care of all publishing aspects unknown to a layman.

Michal Hoftich, the author of `tex4ebook`, was extremely helpful with answering questions regarding producing a nice eBook from the LaTeX sources of the book. I am truly grateful. I couldn't have solved all the issues regarding the eBook on my own.

Many thanks also go to early readers of the manuscript. Their encouragement and their comments have all contributed to the end result. I want to thank Kerstin Gans, Rania Tarazi, Alexandra Kessler, Daniel Liebig, Clemens Scholz and Prof. Dr. Nicolas Neuss.

About the Author

Bernhard Scheffold developed his first successful software in the early 1980s when he contributed to the ORDER timetable management and generation software. During the 80s and early 90s, he studied Physics and Mathematics and acquired a doctorate in natural sciences and a bachelor's degree in mathematics. He has since been working as a software developer in the software industry in various sectors, including finance, health care, administration, embedded, and e-commerce. He is currently a senior software architect with an e-commerce company, helping to create webshops for medium to large-sized companies. His main focus is on integrating various enterprise systems with the webshop and on reliably delivering software changes that provide value to his customers. He lives in Freiburg in the southwest corner of Germany. You can follow his thoughts on Substack at `https://drbernhardscheffold.substack.com`.

www.ingramcontent.com/pod-product-compliance
Lightning Source LLC
Chambersburg PA
CBHW080939240926
51849CB00004BA/499
* 9 7 8 3 9 8 2 7 3 9 2 0 5 *